PERSON TO PERSON

JACK C. RICHARDS   DAVID BYCINA

WITH
MICHAEL BARRETT   ROSAMUNDE BLANCK

PERSON TO PERSON

Communicative speaking and listening skills

TEACHER'S GUIDE FOR BOOKS 1 AND 2

OXFORD UNIVERSITY PRESS
1985

Oxford University Press
200 Madison Avenue   New York,   N.Y. 10016   USA

Walton Street   Oxford OX2 6DP   England

OXFORD is a trademark of Oxford University Press.

Copyright © 1985 by Oxford University Press, Inc.

Library of Congress Cataloging in Publication Data

Richards, Jack C.
Person to Person

1. English language—Text-books for foreign speakers.
I. Bycina, David. II. Title.
PE1128.R46   1985   428.3'4   84-14743
ISBN 0-19-434150-x (v.1)
ISBN 0-19-434152-6 (v.2)
ISBN 0-19-434152-4 (teacher's guide)
ISBN 0-19-434151-8 (book 1 cassettes)
ISBN 0-19-434153-4 (book 2 cassettes)

First published 1985
Fourth impression 1989

All rights reserved. No part of this publication may be reproduced, stored in a retrieval system, or transmitted, in any form or by any means, electronic, mechanical, photocopying, recording, or otherwise, without the prior permission of Oxford University Press.

This book is sold subject to the condition that it shall not, by way of trade or otherwise, be lent, re-sold, hired out, or otherwise circulated without the publisher's prior consent in any form of binding or cover other than that in which it is published and without a similar condition including this condition being imposed on the subsequent purchaser.

Printed in Hong Kong

CONTENTS

Introduction

Components	vi
A Communicative Approach	vi
How a Lesson Works	vii
Notes to the Teacher	ix

Scope and Sequence

Book 1	xi
Book 2	xvi

Teaching Suggestions

Book 1		Book 2	
Unit 1	2	Unit 1	60
Unit 2	8	Unit 2	64
Unit 3	13	Unit 3	67
Unit 4	17	Unit 4	71
Unit 5	21	Unit 5	76
Unit 6	24	Unit 6	78
Unit 7	28	Unit 7	81
Unit 8	32	Unit 8	85
Unit 9	36	Unit 9	89
Unit 10	39	Unit 10	93
Unit 11	41	Unit 11	94
Unit 12	45	Unit 12	97
Unit 13	49	Unit 13	100
Unit 14	52	Unit 14	104
Unit 15	56	Unit 15	107

INTRODUCTION

Components

PERSON TO PERSON consists of

- **Student Books 1 and 2**

Each Student Book contains 15 units. Units 5, 10 and 15 are review units called Variations. All regular units are divided into three sections: a **Conversation**, **Give It a Try** and **Listen to This**. Together the Student Books form a solid listening/speaking course for the intermediate level. However, they can also be used independently of each other.

- **Cassettes**

Each Student Book has two companion cassettes with recordings of:
1. **Conversation**: The opening conversation for each unit (except Variations) is read once at normal speed and then repeated with pauses. Accompanying listening comprehension questions and answers are suggested unit by unit in the Teacher's Guide.
2. **Give It a Try**: The first lines of each numbered section of **Give It a Try** are recorded. These appear in the Student Book as well as in the Teacher's Guide, where the specific lines that have been recorded are marked to show stress and intonation. There are also suggestions for teaching relevant pronunciation points.
3. **Listen to This**: The instructions listed in each unit of the Student Books and the tapescripts at the back of the Student Books are recorded. The tapescripts should not be referred to unless necessary after having heard the recording several times.

- **Teacher's Guide**

This single Teacher's Guide for Books 1 and 2 provides step by step procedures for teaching each unit. It expands on the material in the Student Books by offering additional listening practice based on the opening conversations (See "Listening" under HOW A LESSON WORKS), a pronunciation course (see "Pronunciation"), and suggestions for additional communicative activities in a section entitled, **If You Have Time.** ...

A Communicative Approach

In recent years in language learning there has been a movement away from a focus on grammatical competence as the primary goal towards communicative objectives. This has meant less of an emphasis on grammar drills and grammatical accuracy for its own sake and more of an interest in the processes of communication and in conversational fluency as a goal in conversation teaching. Although grammatical competence is a component of conversational competence, it needs to be supplemented by a number of additional skills which are specific to conversation. Among the most important of these skills and abilities are those relating to the following aspects of conversation.

Topics

In order to be able to take part in conversation, the learner needs to be familiar with a broad range of common topics that occur in everyday conversation. He/She needs to be able to respond to and initiate questions on the situations, events and activities that are commonly referred to during social interaction with speakers of English. This means not only knowing sufficient vocabulary to be able to recognize what is said, but also having something to say about it or add to it.

Speech functions

When people meet they do more than exchange information. They use language to make social interaction possible. This involves the ability to carry out different kinds of conversational tasks and speech functions, such as to greet and acknowledge people, to open and close conversations comfortably, to introduce and develop topics naturally. When we speak to people we not only *say* things, we *do* such things as describe events, feelings, things, ideas, plans and accomplishments; we make requests, offer suggestions, and recommendations; we respond and react to suggestions, opinions, requests, orders and so on. These are the speech functions we use for conversation and which second or foreign language learners need to practice.

To highlight the importance of language functions, consider what happens when they are not taught. As an example, let's take the structure *will*. In grammar courses, students learn that *will* has future meaning. However, *will* actually covers a variety of functions – prediction (*I think it will rain tomorrow.*), warning (*Be careful or you'll fall.*), offer (*I'll do it.*), request (*Will you open the door?*), threat (*Do that again and I'll hit you.*), promise (*I'll take you out for dinner if you pass your exam.*), etc. If students are not aware of these particular uses of *will*, they are likely to think that *will* is interchangeable with other "future" forms, resulting in unnatural or inappropriate utterances. *Are you going to open the door?* is *not* equivalent to *Will you open the door?* And the answer to *What are you doing after work?* cannot be *I will go home.* Just as a single structure can be used to express a number of functions, so can a given function be communicated by a range of grammatical forms. Consider how many ways advice can be given: We can use modals (*Maybe you should/ought to lie down.*), questions, (*Why don't you lie down?/Have you thought about lying down?*), or the conditional (*If I were you, I'd lie down.*).

Unpredictable Forms

When we perform different kinds of speech functions, we usually take part in series of exchanges. For example, I *invite* you to a movie. You *accept* the invitation and *inquire* where and when we will meet. I *suggest* a time and a place. You *accept* my suggestion or *suggest* an alternative. But although this sequence of functions can be predicted once the function of the first utterances in the chain is determined, the actual words and phrases used to express each function cannot be predicted. Conversational competence requires the listener to be able to match and understand the meanings of different sentences and phrases according to where they occur within a sentence.

Appropriate Language

The degree of social distance between speakers influences the forms of address used, what is talked about, and how it is said. A speaker must decide for each conversational interaction, what the relationship between the speaker and hearer is. If both are of equal status and share feelings of rapport and solidarity, this will be marked conversationally by a variety of strategies including choice of address forms, verbal formulae and degrees of directness or indirectness.

Thus in speaking to a professor a student may ask, *Could I possibly see you for a few minutes?* and to a friend, *Hey Joe, got a minute?*

As well as using language that is sufficiently polite or casual for the situation, we must also express speech functions according to the conventions of English. We can greet a person in English with *How are you?*, but although the expressions *Are you well?* and *How is your health?* are both English, they are not customarily used as greetings. A great deal of conversational language is in this sense idiomatic and conventional.

Mutually created

Conversation is a two-way process. Both participants share the responsibility of maintaining the flow of talk and of making their contributions comprehensible and relevant. This means that there is a need for speakers to give ongoing feedback to each other.

Conversational competence thus involves an integration of grammatical and the other kinds of skills noted above, and practice in this is what *Person to Person* is all about.

The functions and topics included in *Person to Person* are based on a selection from the Threshold level decided on by the Council of Europe in its study of the communicative needs of adult users of English as a second language as well as consideration of the grammar points needed by students at the basic and intermediate levels that are compatible with them. The topics and functions that are introduced in each unit of Book 1 are reintroduced in each corresponding unit of Book 2 at a more advanced level. A complete listing of functions and topics appears in the Scope and Sequence Chart on pages xi–xx.

How a lesson works

Conversation

Each regular unit in the Student Book begins with a conversation which has been recorded on the cassette twice, the first time at regular speed and the second time with pauses. Prepare students for the topic and for new vocabulary using the suggestions in this Teacher's Guide under "Setting the Scene" and "Vocabulary." Then, if you wish to use the conversation for listening practice, follow the steps described below.
Time: approximately 20 min.

Vocabulary

The Teacher's Guide suggests vocabulary items for presentation in conjunction with the opening **Conversation** and the **Listen to This** sections. We have placed "Vocabulary" before "Listening." However, it is up to you to choose if and when to introduce new vocabulary items. You may wish to postpone the introduction of new vocabulary until after students have heard the conversation once. This will encourage them to listen to the whole utterance and get the message from that whole, rather than to listen for individual words. Tell students to keep listening even if they hear a word or two they don't understand. Tell them that you will work with vocabulary after the first listening.

When possible, have a picture or example of the item being introduced. Ask *Do you know the English word for this?* If no one does, tell them what it is and either write it on the board yourself or ask a student to do so. When it is not possible to illustrate a vocabulary item, write the item on the board. First, ask the students if anyone can give a definition or an example to show they understand the word. If not, you can supply a definition or demonstration. Alternately, if you and your students have the same native language, you might choose to simply translate the word, or, if bilingual dictionaries are acceptable in your class, allow students to look up the word or phrase.

Listening

Especially for the first few units, assure the students they will have several opportunities to hear the conversation. They will hear it both at normal speed and with pauses. They will also be able to read it afterwards.

1. Play the tape or read the conversation a first time. If you are reading, use normal conversational speed.
2. Have students prepare answer sheets for the questions you will write on the board:
   a. b. c.
   Assure students that these will not be collected. They do not have to answer in full sentences. Give an example if necessary.
3. While students are preparing their answer sheets, write the questions given in the Teacher's Guide on the board.
4. At this point, students may be able to answer some of the questions because they have heard the conversation once. Give them a chance to make notes privately if it seems appropriate.
5. Now, let students hear the conversation again, this time with pauses. Encourage them to listen for the information they need to answer the questions on the board.
6. Give students time to write down their answers. Remind them that they do not have to write complete sentences.
7. Have students check their answers with one or two classmates. Encourage them to discuss their reasons for answering as they did.
8. Play the tape or read the conversation again. Let students check their notes as they listen.
9. Check the answers. This can be done in a number of ways:
   a. Students can compare answers with classmates.
   b. As the students are writing, you can walk around the room to observe what they are writing. You can put a mark next to any wrong answers so that the students will know to pay special attention to those sections as they listen to the conversation again.
10. Play or read the conversation again at normal speed. If there are any parts students are having special difficulty understanding, play or read them with pauses.
11. Final check.
    a. You can ask the class for the answers and write them on the board.
    b. You can ask students to volunteer to write the answers on the board.
12. Let the students read the script in their books as they listen again.

Give It a Try

The many exchanges that together made up the opening conversation are examined one by one in the numbered sections of **Give It a Try**.

Play or read the conversational exchange. Follow the suggestions in the Teacher's Guide for teaching the pronunciation point featured in that segment. These points form the basis of a pronunciation course developed throughout this Guide. See "Pronunciation" below for fuller explanation.

Then, focus on the points of culture, grammar and usage highlighted in boxes labeled "Of Interest."

After this, have students do the practice activities that follow in pairs or in small groups.
Time: approximately 15 minutes for each numbered section.

Listen to This

All regular units end with a task-based listening section called **Listen to This**. These are recorded on the cassette. Follow the procedures suggested below for guiding students through this section as they listen to the conversations and perform the appropriate tasks, then verify their information.

Time: 20–30 min.
1. Have students look at the instructions to **Listen to This** in their books, read the questions and look at the illustrations so they know what to listen for. Go over any questions they may have.
2. Play the cassette or read the tapescript (at the back of the Student Books) at normal conversational speed. Students listen and write their answers.
3. Replay the cassette (you will have to rewind it) or read the tapescript again as students check their information.
4. If there are any parts students are having special difficulty with, play or read them again.
5. Check answers using any of the suggestions given in the preceding section. You may also allow students to look at the tapescript while they listen again.

As with all procedures mentioned in this course, these are suggestions. Adapt them in accordance with your own preferences and the needs of your students. For example, you may wish to vary the number of times you replay or reread the listening sections to your students. You may want to add more pauses. Feel free to experiment as you find what works best for your class.

If You Have Time...

Each unit of the Teacher's Guide ends with **If You Have Time...**, a section that provides suggestions for additional communicative activities.
Time: 10-20 min.

Notes to the Teacher

Grammar and Usage

Person to Person is not meant to be a grammar text and should not be used as one. The authors assume that basic grammar has been taught and learned either in previous years or in other classes and that here the students need practice in using that grammar in a natural conversational setting. However, grammar is carefully controlled so that, as far as possible, the major aspects of English grammar are carefully reviewed in natural contexts. The units progress in grammatical difficulty, although you could do them out of sequence if your class can handle it, and Book 2 extends and builds on the grammatical patterns used in Book 1. When unusual uses of a grammatical structure are used, explanations and brief exercises are provided in the Teacher's Guide. These are usually found in **Give It a Try** and can be done as quick drills at the beginning of the section. A summary of the grammar points involved in each unit of the student book appears in the Scope and Sequence Chart that follows this introduction.

Pronunciation

By following the pronunciation points in this Teacher's Guide, you will give your students an awareness of those features of the sound system of American English which will be most useful to them as listeners as well as speakers of English. These are: intonation, sentence stress, rhythm, blending and reduction.

Let's start with sentence stress and intonation. Speakers use stress and intonation to mark the words they want to highlight, to signal the end of a thought unit and to indicate such things as whether that unit is part of a series or a completed thought, whether it is a statement, a Wh-question, a yes-no question, or a request.

Intonation patterns:

request: Could I have your name, please?

statement: It's Paine.

Wh-question: How do you spell that?

series: It's P A I N E.

yes-no question: Do you live in Chicago?

This leads us to blending and reduction. Words which are not given strong stress are often said quickly, "swallowed," or otherwise altered. *What did he* becomes /Wuh-de/; *Could you* becomes /Cu-juh/; *did she* becomes /che/; and so on. This is because English is a stress-timed language: In contrast to many languages where each syllable a speaker says takes the same length of time, in English only those syllables that are stressed are said slowly. When listening to a rapid stream of speech, students of English sometimes find it hard to recognize even the words that they know because they are unfamiliar with their unstressed (or reduced) forms. Thus they may know the words *did*, *you*, *eat* and *yet*, but a simple sentence like *Did you eat yet?*, rapidly said, /Jeet chet?/ may be a total mystery.

Person to Person addresses these features of blending and reduction as well as stress, rhythm and intonation throughout the Teacher's Guide. To avoid the need for specialized phonetic symbols, the transcriptions used in this book are based on regular English spellings. For a complete listing of pronunciation points, see the Scope and Sequence Chart.

Pair work

Person to Person is based on paired and small group activities which maximize each student's opportunity to speak in class. Clear language models and guided exercises enable pairs to work alone productively. The elements of real communication are simulated in role-plays, many of which involve an "information gap," in which one student has information that the other one needs. Even scripted role-plays are made more realistic by using a "split dialog" format in which Student A does not see student B's lines and vice versa.

```
Student A
A: My name's __ (full name) __ .
B: _____ .
A: Sorry, what's your first name again?
                  last
                  name
B: _____ .
```

```
Student B
A: _____ .
B: Hi, I'm __ (full name) __ .
A: _____ ?
B: __ (name) __ .
```

As students practice in pairs or small groups, you can walk around the room and listen to them. In many instances you will hear incorrect usage, hesitancy, unclear pronunciation, and other things that you might want students to work on. Note those areas needing work. Don't step in at the instant you hear an error because that might inhibit students. It is important to allow them some time for free practice. After students have had a chance to become comfortable with the practice, you can offer guidance so that they can improve what they have done.

Try to establish yourself as a resource rather than a police officer. There may be times when students get stuck because they do not have a vocabulary item needed to proceed. Encourage them to call you over to help.

In many instances, the Teacher's Guide suggests that one or two pairs of students perform their conversations in front of the class. As you walk around during their practice time, you can be deciding which pairs to choose.

SCOPE AND SEQUENCE CHART BOOK ONE

UNIT 1 Nice to meet you.

Functions	Topics	Pronunciation	Grammar
1. Introducing youself 2. Asking for repetition 3. Asking someone's occupation 4. Asking for more information (1) 5. Asking for more information (2) 6. Conversational openings 7. Introducing yourself – more formally	Greetings. Introductions. First and last names. Occupations. Courses of study.	1. statement intonation 2. rising intonation to request repetition 3. sentence stress 4. intonation of *Wh*-questions 5. sentence stress 6. intonation of tag questions 7. blending of *meet you*	Present and present progressive tenses. Contractions with *be*. *Wh*-question: *what*. Tag questions. Indefinite article with occupations. Verb + preposition: *work for*, *go to*. Personal pronouns. Possessive adjective: *my*. Adverbs of degree: *very*, *really*.

UNIT 2 We'll have to fill out some forms.

Functions	Topics	Pronunciation	Grammar
1. Names 2. Addresses 3. Telephone numbers 4. Occupations 5. Asking personal questions – more politely 6. Calling information	Names. Addresses. Telephone numbers. Occupations. Savings account and credit card applications. Apartment rentals.	1. series intonation 2. saying building numbers in addresses 3. saying telephone numbers 4. review of *Wh*-question and statement intonation 5. rising intonation for requests 6. answering the telephone	Polite requests with modals: *can*, *could*, *may*, *would*. *Wh*-questions: *where*, *how*. *yes-no* questions. Negation. Contractions with *not*. Contractions with *would*. Prepositions in addresses: *at*, *on*, *in*. Possessive adjectives: *your*, *his*.

UNIT 3 So, tell me about your family.

Functions	Topics	Pronunciation	Grammar
1. Do you have any brothers or sisters? 2. How old are they? 3. What do they do? 4. Are you married? 5. Extension: Do you have any children? 6. Getting information about someone's family	Family. Age. Occupations. Surveys.	1. intonation of *yes-no* questions 2. intonation of clauses in a series 3. review of series intonation 4. review of question and statement intonation 5. general review of intonation 6. review of rising intonation for requests	Embedded *Wh*-questions with modals. *yes-no* questions. *have/have got*. Contractions with *have*. Comparisons and superlatives of one-syllable adjectives. Pronouns: *other*, *other one*. Sentence coordination: *and*, *but*.

UNIT 4 Hurry up. We're late.

Functions	Topics	Pronunciation	Grammar
1. Asking where things are 2. Asking where things are – more politely 3. Asking where things are – outside 4. Telling time 5. Starting and finishing times 6. Opening and closing times	Clothing. Furniture. Street locations. Opening and closing times.	1. stress in NOUN-NOUN constructions 2. review of rising intonation for *yes-no* questions 3. intonation of introductory expressions 4. review of rising-falling intonation 5. sentence stress 6. review of sentence stress	Embedded *Wh*-questions with modals. *Wh*-questions: *when*. Negative *yes-no* questions. *It* in time expressions. NOUN-NOUN constructions. Prepositions of place: *down, on, near, opposite, at the end/beginning, before, between, around, to the right/left, in the middle of, past.*

UNIT 5 Variations

Functions	Topics	Pronunciation	Grammar
(Review of Units 1, 2, 3 and 4)	Subscription forms. Airline schedules. Kitchen accessories. TV quiz programs. Countries and capitals. Famous places and people.	(Review of Units 1, 2, 3 and 4)	(Review of Units 1, 2, 3 and 4)

UNIT 6 Are you doing anything tonight?

Functions	Topics	Pronunciation	Grammar
1. Informal invitations: accepting 2. Informal invitations: declining 3. Beginning an invitation 4. Suggesting another time 5. Setting the time and place 6. More formal invitations: accepting and declining 7. Setting another time – more formally 8. Setting the time and the place – more formally	Dating. Recreational activities. Time.	1. review of question and statement intonation 2. blending of *want to* and *have to* 3. special intonation 4. stressed and reduced forms of *can* and *can't* 5. rhythm 6. auxiliaries in terminal position 7. blending of *could you* 8. blending of *would you*	Questions with modals: *could, would, should.* Embedded *yes-no* questions. Present progressive with future meaning. Past progressive. *Have (got) to.* Contractions with *have. Would like* + infinitive. Contractions with *would.*

Scope and sequence chart Book One

UNIT 7 Which way is the post office?

Functions	Topics	Pronunciation	Grammar
1. Asking directions: responding negatively 2. Asking more politely: responding negatively 3. Asking more politely: responding positively. 4. Giving simple directions 5. Giving longer directions (1) 6. Giving longer directions (2) 7. Confirming and correcting	Street directions.	1. intonation for politeness 2. review of auxiliaries in terminal position 3. special intonation 4. review of stress, rhythm and intonation 5. unstressed words 6. intonation in a series of directions 7. special intonation	Polite requests with modals. Embedded *Wh*-questions with modals. Imperatives. Prepositions of place. *Until* + clause.

UNIT 8 Do you like jazz?

Functions	Topics	Pronunciation	Grammar
1. Likes and dislikes (1) 2. Likes and dislikes (2) 3. Agreeing with someone's likes 4. Agreeing with someone's dislikes 5. Disagreeing with someone's likes 6. Disagreeing with someone's dislikes 7. What kind of _____ do you like? 8. Favorites 9. Preferences	Entertainment. Popular music. Sports. Food. Hobbies. Movies.	1. review of question and statement intonation 2. special intonation 3. how stress conveys meaning 4. how stress conveys meaning 5. how stress conveys meaning 6. review of sentence stress and meaning 7. blending of *kind of* 8. reduced form of *your* 9. contrastive stress and intonation	*Like* + gerund. Adverbs of degree: *very much, at all, especially, sort of*. Superlative adverb *best*. Short answers with *too, so, either, neither*.

UNIT 9 And what did you do then?

Functions	Topics	Pronunciation	Grammar
1. Talking about personal history 2. Clarifying information 3. Being specific 4. Length of time 5. What next?	Personal history. Resumes. Education. Work experience.	1. blending of *did you* 2. intonation questions 3. reduced form of *for* 4. review of *did you* 5. blending of *what did you*	Simple past. Adverbs of place: *here, there*. Adverbs of sequence: *first, then, after that. After/before* + gerund phrase/clause. *About, for, ago,* in time expressions. *When* + clause.

UNIT 10 Variations

Functions	Topics	Pronunciation	Grammar
(Review of Units 6, 7, 8 and 9)	Dating. Street directions. Personal history.	(Review of Units 6, 7, 8 and 9)	(Review of Units 6, 7, 8 and 9)

UNIT 11 And what would you like?

Functions	Topics	Pronunciation	Grammar
In a restaurant: 1. Expressing wants among friends/family 2. Speaking to a waiter/waitress 3. Specifying wants 4. Asking about wants 5. Asking about other wants 6. Offering service At someone's house for dinner: 7. Offering and accepting food	Food. Menus. Shopping lists.	1. blending of *going to* 2. special use of rising intonation 3. blending of *would you* 4. polite intonation 5. review of intonation 6. review of intonation 7. stress and intonation	Future forms: *will, going to. Would like.* Questions with modals. Contractions with *will* and *would.* Quantifiers: *some, any. A piece/an order of* + noun. *Anything else.*

UNIT 12 How have you been?

Functions	Topics	Pronunciation	Grammar
1. Greetings 2. Asking about others 3. Gossiping 4. Reacting 5. Ending the conversation (1) 6. Ending the conversation (2) 7. Greeting people – more formally 8. Ending the conversation – more formally	News about others. Good and bad news.	1. emphatic intonation 2. special intonation 3. sentence stress 4. stress in two-word verbs 5. blending of *got to* 6. reduced form of *to* 7. contrastive stress 8. contrastive stress	Present perfect tense. Simple past. Present progressive. *Have (got) to.* Verb + preposition: *hear about, ask for.*

Scope and sequence chart　Book One

UNIT 13　What did the person look like?

Functions	Topics	Pronunciation	Grammar
1. Describing people (1) 2. Describing people (2) 3. Asking about age 4. Describing hair and eyes 5. Describing clothing 6. Describing things	Height. Weight. Size. Age. Hair. Clothing.	1. blending of *What did he* 2. review of reduced form of *he* 3. reduced form of *his* 4. review of reduced forms 5. reduced form of *and* 6. stress in noun phrases	Simple past and past progressive tenses. Adjectives. Adverbs of degree: *very, fairly, pretty, kind of, sort of, rather, around, about*.

UNIT 14　Have you ever been to Japan?

Functions	Topics	Pronunciation	Grammar
1. Past experiences 2. Asking for a description or opinion (1) 3. Asking for a description or opinion (2) 4. Comparing (1) 5. Things to see 6. Comparing (2) 7. Comparing (3)	Vacations. Visiting other cities.	1. review of stress, intonation and rhythm 2. review of stress and rhythm 3. intonation with *but* 4. review of sentence stress 5. stress and intonation to highlight important ideas 6. review of sentence stress 7. review of stress, intonation and rhythm	Present perfect and past tenses. Comparisons and superlatives of adjectives. *Than* after comparative adjectives. Negative comparisons: *not so/as ... as*. Quantifiers: *lots of, many, some*. Comparative and superlative quantifiers: *more* and *most*. Adverbs of degree.

UNIT 15　Variations

Functions	Topics	Pronunciation	Grammar
(Review of Units 11, 12, 13 and 14)	Food. Friends. Medical histories. Vacations. Cities.	(Review of Units 11, 12, 13 and 14)	(Review of Units 11, 12, 13 and 14)

SCOPE AND SEQUENCE CHART   BOOK TWO

UNIT 1   Haven't we met before?

Functions	Topics	Pronunciation	Grammar
1. Reintroducing yourself (1) 2. Reintroducing yourself (2) 3. Identifying someone and being told you are mistaken 4. Asking whether you've met before 5. Introducing another person 6. Talking about occupations 7. Introducing another person more formally	Names. Occupations.	1. review of *Wh*-question intonation 2. review of statement intonation 3. review of *yes-no* question intonation 4. review of tag question intonation 5. review of contrastive stress 6. review of intonation 7. reduced form of *to*	Present perfect and past tenses. *Wh*-questions. Negative *yes-no* questions. Tag questions. Contractions with *be* and *have*. *think/believe* + *that* clause.

UNIT 2   Would you mind telling me?

Functions	Topics	Pronunciation	Grammar
1. Confirming information 2. Asking questions in formal situations 3. Asking for clarification 4. Asking for further information 5. Closing an interview	Job interviews. Education. Work experience. Job benefits.	1. special intonation 2. stress and intonation in connected sentences 3. review of *Wh*-question and statement intonation 4. stress and rhythm 5. stress and intonation	Present perfect and past tenses. Polite requests with modals. Embedded *Wh*-questions with modals. Embedded *yes-no* questions. *would like* + infinitive. Contractions with *would*. *look forward to* + gerund.

UNIT 3   Isn't he the one who . . . ?

Functions	Topics	Pronunciation	Grammar
1. Asking who someone is 2. Asking about someone 3. Asking about someone's personality 4. Identifying someone 5. Asking about personal details	Ways of identifying people. Nationalities. Occupations. Personality. Family.	1. blending in *Do you* 2. review of reduced form of *he* 3. blending of *What's he* 4. blending of *Is he* 5. rhythm	Embedded *Wh*-questions. Embedded *yes-no* questions. Restrictive relative clauses. Relative pronoun *whose*. Adjectival phrases. Adverbs of degree: *very, pretty, rather*.

UNIT 4   Where exactly is it?

Functions	Topics	Pronunciation	Grammar
1. Asking where facilities and services are located 2. Locating streets 3. Asking for specific locations 4. Identifying buildings by appearance and location 5. Asking where inside a building something is located 6. Asking about opening/closing times (1) 7. Asking about opening/closing times (2)	Locations inside and outside. Hotels. Department stores.	1. blending of *Is there* 2. contrastive stress 3. sentence stress 4. stress in NOUN-NOUN combinations 5. review 6. stress when telling time 7. two ways to say *the*	*get/have* + noun phrase + past participle. Prepositions in addresses: *in, at*. Prepositions of place: *past, after, before, opposite, across from, near, next to*. Adverbs of place: *upstairs, downstairs*. Prepositions of time: *till, until, from...to...* Prepositions of time and date: *in the evening, on the weekend*.

UNIT 5   Variations

Functions	Topics	Pronunciation	Grammar
(Review of Units 1, 2, 3 and 4)	Introductions. Personal information. Street locations.	(Review of Units 1, 2, 3 and 4)	(Review of Units 1, 2, 3 and 4)

UNIT 6   You'd better get some rest.

Functions	Topics	Pronunciation	Grammar
1. Asking what the matter is 2. Giving tentative advice (1) 3. Giving tentative advice (2) 4. Giving advice (1) 5. Giving advice not to do something 6. Giving advice (2)	Health complaints and remedies.	1. special intonation 2. tone of voice 3. tone of voice 4. reduced form of *you'd better* 5. intonation for emphasis 6. intonation in complex sentences	*should/ought to/had better*. Present contrary to fact conditional sentences: *I / were you, I would.... What I would do is* + verb.

UNIT 7 Do I need to ...?

Functions	Topics	Pronunciation	Grammar
1. Asking the procedure 2. Asking what the requirements are 3. Asking whether something is permitted/recommended 4. Asking when it is possible to do something 5. Asking about rules/regulations	American universities. Application procedures. Rules and regulations. Driving regulations. Recipes.	1. intonation of sequential items 2. *to* in terminal position 3. *to* before vowels and consonants 4. rhythm 5. intonation of short answers	Imperatives. *have to/need to.* Embedded *yes-no* questions. *can/will be able to.* Contractions with *not: can't, aren't. be allowed/be permitted* + infinitive. Adverbs of sequence: *first, then, after that.*

UNIT 8 What do you think?

Functions	Topics	Pronunciation	Grammar
1. Asking and giving opinions 2. Agreeing with an opinion 3. Expressing a negative opinion 4. Disagreeing 5. Qualifying a statement	Television. Gun control.	1. intonation of *if* clauses 2. intonation in sentences with more than one main thought group 3. review of intonation in sentences with more than one thought group 4. special intonation 5. review of intonation	Gerund phrases as subjects. Verb + preposition: *think of/feel about.* Sentence coordination: *and, but.* Adverbs of degree: *pretty, too, extremely, very.* Determiners: *much, many, enough.*

UNIT 9 What did he do next?

Functions	Topics	Pronunciation	Grammar
1. Asking whether someone has done something 2. Talking about habitual actions in the past 3. Describing past events in sequence 4. Describing concurrent past events 5. Describing what someone has been doing	Past history. Work experience.	1. special intonation 2. blending of *Has he* 3. review of stress, rhythm and intonation 4. review of intonation 5. contrastive stress	Present perfect and present perfect progressive tenses. Simple past and past progressive tenses. *used to. while, when, as soon as, after* + gerund phrase/clause. Adverbs of time: *yet, already, ever, before, since then.*

UNIT 10 Variations

Functions	Topics	Pronunciation	Grammar
(Review of Units 6, 7, 8 and 9)	Customs. Personal problems. Personal history. Recipes. National issues.	(Review of Units 6, 7, 8 and 9)	(Review of Units 6, 7, 8 and 9)

UNIT 11 What are you going to do?

Functions	Topics	Pronunciation	Grammar
1. Asking about future plans (1) 2. Asking about future plans (2) 3. Asking about future plans (3) 4. Describing changes in plans 5. Explaining possibilities	Future plans: immediate and long range.	1. blending of *going to* reviewed 2. review of intonation 3. blending of *What are you* 4. blending of *going to* reviewed 5. contrastive stress	*going to* + verb. Present progressive to express the future. Past progressive. Present and past perfect. *plan/intend* + infinitive. *think of* + gerund. Future conditional sentences: *If I get a scholarship, I'll....*

UNIT 12 Did you hear what happened?

Functions	Topics	Pronunciation	Grammar
1. Responding to good and bad news 2. Suggesting how something probably occurred 3. Saying what someone should have done 4. Suggesting a course of action	Good and bad news. Accidents and illnesses. Advice. Probability.	1. intonation choices 2. blending of *must have* 3. blending of *should have* 4. review of stress, rhythm and intonation	*know/hear* + relative clause. Perfect modals: *must have, should have, ought to have.* Future conditional sentences: *If he stays in the hospital, he should be able to avoid complications.*

UNIT 13 What's this for?

Functions	Topics	Pronunciation	Grammar
1. Describing what objects are used for 2. Explaining the reasons for certain features 3. Explaining how to do things (1) 4. Explaining how to do things (2) 5. Describing where things were made and what they are made of 6. Finding out whether something can be done	Household appliances. Operating instructions. Procedures. Care of clothing and other things.	1. stressed and reduced forms of *for* 2. blending of *Why is it* 3. intonation to show connections 4. review of stress in two word verbs 5. review of stress and rhythm 6. review of the reduced form of *can*	*for* + gerund/*to* + infinitive to express purpose. Passive voice. Present perfect passive. Adverbs of sequence.

UNIT 14 What did they say about it?

Functions	Topics	Pronunciation	Grammar
1. Asking about what someone said (1) 2. Asking about what someone said (2) 3. Asking about what someone said (3) 4. Asking about what someone said (4) 5. Reporting recommendations 6. Reporting information from a book	Vacations. Travel. Accommodations.	1. review of stress, intonation and rhythm 2. stress 3. blending of *Did she* 4. blending of *Did you ask* 5. blending of *What does it*	Reported speech. *say/tell/recommend/suggest/advise* + complement. Modals: *would, could, might*. Verb + preposition: *say about, ask about*.

UNIT 15 Variations

Functions	Topics	Pronunciation	Grammar
(Review of Units 11, 12, 13 and 14)	Weddings. Cars. Bad news. Travel.	(Review of Units 11, 12, 13 and 14)	(Review of Units 11, 12, 13 and 14)

BOOK ONE

UNIT 1

Nice to meet you

Setting the Scene

Prepare students for the opening conversation. Have them turn to the first page of Unit 1 and look at the photograph while covering the conversation with half a sheet of paper. (This is done so that the conversation can be used as a listening exercise. Assure students that they will be able to see the conversation later.) Say: *We're all at the party, but there are some people I don't know. I walk up to someone. What do I say?* (*Hi,, my name is _ _ _ _ _ _.*) Ask: *What does the other person say? What other things can we say? What do we talk about?* Be sure to act out some of the non-verbal communication that goes with the situation: a smile, a nod of the head, a handshake, etc.

Vocabulary

(See the Introduction for a discussion of vocabulary.)
  Your students may be unfamiliar with these words or other vocabulary items you may select. Introduce them now or after they hear the conversation once.

graduate student: a person who has completed a four-year undergraduate degree (a B.A. or B.S.) at a college or university in the U.S. and is now taking further courses, usually for a master's degree (M.A.) or a doctorate (Ph.D.)

section: as used here, a division or part of a company

by the way: a common phrase used to introduce or change a topic of conversation

It's not bad: It's OK. (a positive response that does not show very much enthusiasm)

Listening

1. Play the tape or read the conversation at normal speed.
2. Have students prepare answer sheets for the questions you will write on the board. (Items a–f). Assure students that these will not be collected. They do not have to answer in full sentences, just one or two words. Do the first one on the board as an example:
   a. *party*   or   *at a party*
3. Write these questions on the board:
   a. Where are the people? (*at a party*)
   b. What is the woman's name: Betty Marshall, Bev Marshall or Viv Marsh? (*Bev Marshall*)
   c. What does she do? (*studies/graduate student at Columbia*)
   d. What's the man's name: Jim Harris, Tim Maris or Jim Carras? (*Jim Harris*)
   e. Where does he work? (*Citibank//in the International Section*)
   f. Does he like his job? (*maybe/hard to say/pretty well*)
4. Give the students a moment to write any answers they already can. Remind them that they do not need to write full sentences.
5. Now let the students hear the conversation again. This time leave pauses between speakers.
6. Give the students time to write their answers. Again, remind them that they do not have to write complete sentences.
7. Have the students check their answers with one or two classmates.
8. Let the students hear the conversation again. Have them check their answers as they listen.
9. Check the answers.
   a. Students can compare answers with classmates.
   b. As the students are writing, you can walk around the room to observe what they are writing. This will give you a good idea of where there may be problems. It will also allow you to see which students have the answers and which may need more listening time. You can mark an **x** next to any wrong answers so that students will pay special attention to those sections of the conversation.
10. Play or read the conversation again at normal speed. If necessary, play them with pauses.
11. Do a final check.
    a. You can ask the class for the answers and write them on the board, or you can ask students to volunteer to write the answers on the board.
12. Let students read the conversation in their books. Then let them hear the conversation again while they are looking at their books.

GIVE IT A TRY

1. Introducing yourself

▶ My name's Jim Harris.

▷ Hi, I'm Bev Marshall.

Pronunciation: statement intonation

1. Play the cassette or read the dialog. Then say or play each line and have students repeat.
2. Play or read the model again.
3. On the blackboard, copy the intonation contour shown above without the words. (If necessary, you can add the words later.)
4. Repeat the lines while tracing the intonation contour with your hand or a pointer.
5. Now have students say the lines.
6. If they have difficulty with the intonation:
   a. Hum each line, drawing attention to the rise and fall of the voice.
   b. (While humming) use your hand to show the rise and fall.
   c. Write the words on the board with their intonation contours.
7. You may wish to tell your students that the intonation pattern they have just practiced is called rising-falling and that it is used at the end of statements (and *Wh*-questions).
8. Model and have students repeat the alternative sentences in their books in the same way.

Practice

a. Walk up to a student and role-play the above lines. Draw attention to your non-verbal behavior (smiling, inclining forward slightly, shaking hands).
b. Have students practice in pairs. (see Introduction.) As you walk around and monitor their performance, remind them not to forget the non-verbal part of the interaction.

2. Asking for repetition

▶ Sorry, what's your first name again?

▷ It's Beverly, but please call me Bev.

Pronunciation: rising intonation to request repetition

Follow the procedure outlined in the preceding section to teach the intonation of these sentences. Note the unusual use of rising intonation in the above *Wh*-question. It is used here to indicate a request for *repetition*. You may wish to point out to your students how this differs from the normal intonation of a *Wh*-question.

normal *Wh*-question   **asking for repetition**

What's your name?   What's your name?

Of Interest

a. In the United States, people use first names right away when they meet people of their own age and status. You can tell your students that if they are unsure, it is safest to use the polite title, *Mr. Miss, Mrs., Ms*.*, etc. and wait for the other person to suggest using his/her first name. Alternatively, if they are addressed by title, they can suggest that the other person use their first name.
b. In asking someone to repeat what they have said, we often use the past tense. Jim could have said, *What **was** your name again?*

Practice

a. Choose one student to model the conversation with you. Illustrate to the class how you and your partner are each covering the other person's lines.
b. Model the conversation using the "read and look up" technique:
Look at the text to be read aloud. Then, when ready to speak, look at the person(s) you are talking to and say your line (or part of your line). Look down at the page again for the next part, and, again, look up while saying the line. The reader's eyes should never be in the book while he/she is speaking. This will help students to role-play more naturally. At the same time, it will improve their reading fluency by requiring them to take in phrases, rather than read word by word.
c. Switch parts and model it again.
d. Have students practice the conversation with their partners and then, when they feel comfortable, with several people around them. Circulate among students, providing help as needed.

* *Ms./miz/* is the feminine equivalent of the masculine title *Mr*. Many women in the United States use it in preference to the titles *Miss* or *Mrs.*, which establish marital status. It is commonly used in business situations when the woman to be addressed has not indicated a preference for another title.

3. Asking someone's occupation

▶ What do you do, Bev?

▷ Well, I'm a grad student at Columbia.

▶ Oh, are you?

▷ And what about you, Jim?

▶ I work for Citibank.

▷ Oh, do you?

Pronunciation: sentence stress

In every sentence, there is at least one syllable that gets strong stress: That is, it is said louder, held longer and is sometimes pronounced at a higher pitch. Generally the words which receive stress are content words (nouns, verbs, adjectives, adverbs) and *Wh-*question words. The last stressed syllable in an utterance is the one that receives the greatest stress. In two of the sentences above, the strongest stress falls on the auxillary verbs, which is unusual. A filled-in circle (•) has been used to indicate stress in this Teacher's Guide.
1. Play the cassette or read the whole model.
2. Then say or play each line and have students repeat.
3. Write the dialog on the board and indicate on the first three lines the syllables that receive sentence stress.
4. Using a pointer or pen, tap each syllable on the board, hitting the stressed syllables with greater force.
5. Have students repeat the lines.
6. Now model the last three lines and ask students to tell you which syllables they hear strong stress on. As they tell you the correct answers, mark the appropriate syllables.

Of Interest

1. When people in the United States first meet, they frequently ask each other their occupations and talk a little about their work.
2. The questions *Oh, are you?* and *Oh, do you?* show polite interest and are, obviously, very useful. Note that *are* and *you* correspond to the previous speaker's statement.

Practice

a. Ask students for other possible occupations. Write the words on the board. Model them orally and have students repeat.
b. Model the above exchange again using two of the new vocabulary words.
c. Have students divide into pairs and practice both parts of the conversation while you circulate, providing help as needed. Remind them to "read and look up."

4. Asking for more information (1)

▶ What are you studying?

▷ Business.

OR

▶ What do you do there exactly?

▷ I'm a secretary.

Pronunciation: intonation of *Wh-*questions

The intonation of *Wh-*questions is like that of statements. The voice rises and falls on the last stressed syllable.
  Follow the procedure for teaching intonation used earlier in this unit. Have students practice this model. Then practice saying the alternate sentence.

Vocabulary

Personnel Department: the section of a company that deals with employees, their hiring, training, etc.

Public Relations Department: the section of a company that deals with its public image and community relations.

Practice 1 and 2

a. Model the exchange with a student, using the "read and look up" technique. Then switch roles.
b. Have students do the conversations with several people around them, switching parts and partners when they feel comfortable. Walk around the room, making suggestions and giving help as needed.

Nice to meet you.

Extension

Call on different pairs of students to practice their dialogs while other students listen. After each pair has finished, ask questions such as *What school does she/he go to? What is she/he studying? What company does she/he work for? What does she/he do?*

Practice 3

a. Have each student practice the dialog with two or three different partners, switching roles with each partner.
b. Ask several students to give information about some of their partners.

5. Asking for more information (2)

▶ I'm a student.

▷ Oh, really? What school do you go to?

▶ I go to Columbia.

OR

▶ I'm an engineer.

▷ Oh, really? What company do you work for?

▶ (I work for) Nissan.

Pronunciation: sentence stress

In the questions *What school do you go to?* and *What company do you work for?* the stress is on *school* and *company* because these words are the focus of interest in the questions. (In other contexts, the stress might fall on the verbs *go* and *work* or even on the pronoun *you* if people are being contrasted. Each change in stress causes a slight change in meaning.) Follow the procedure for teaching stress presented earlier in the Unit. Then have students practice saying these models.

Practice 1 and 2

a. Choose a person in the class who in real life is a student and model the first dialog. Then choose a student who has a job and do the same. If none of the students has a job, let them choose one of the occupations listed and practiced earlier. (p. 3 of the Student Book)
b. Have students practice the dialog with several members of the class, using the "read and look up" technique.

6. Conversational openings

▶ (It's a) great party, isn't it?

▷ Yeah, really.

Pronunciation: intonation of tag questions

Tag questions asked with a rising-falling intonation are intended as statements of fact. The speaker expects the listener to agree with him/her.

Model and have students practice this intonation pattern. (See Introduction for procedure.)

Draw attention to the two responses: *Yeah, really* and *Yes, it is.* Ask students which is more informal. Discuss where it could/could not be used.

> **Of Interest**
>
> Strangers often begin a conversation by commenting on some aspect of their immediate circumstances. For example, during their first English class they might begin by mentioning the size of the class, commenting on the teacher or the room, etc.

Practice

a. Have the students look at the first picture in the book. Ask: *Where does the conversation take place? Why are the people there?* etc.
b. Model the first dialog with a student. Then ask the class for other appropriate conversation openings.
c. Follow the same procedure for the other two pictures.
d. Divide the class into pairs and have each pair choose any two pictures. Ask them to develop and practice their own openings for each.
e. Have several pairs of students perform their opening conversations for the class. The rest of the class can comment on appropriateness.

7. Introducing yourself – more formally

▶ Let me introduce myself. My name's Robert Andrews.

▶ How do you do? I'm Jean Rivers.

▶ It's very nice to meet you.

Pronunciation: blending of *meet you*

In normal rapid speech, *meet you* is often blended to sound like /me-chu/.

1. Play or read the dialog and have students repeat each line.
2. Then write on the board: *It's nice to meet ch you.*
3. Pointing to the *ch*, say /me-chu/. Have students repeat.
4. Tell students that it is not necessary for them to pronounce the /ch/, especially if they are speaking slowly, but knowing that it occurs will help them understand native speakers in rapid conversation.

Of Interest

1. In certain business situations, formal social situations, or in meeting with people who are older, people frequently use a more formal type of introduction. In these situations, it is better to use titles such as Mr., Mrs., etc. unless the other person suggests that you use his/her first name.
2. The answer to *How do you do?* is *How do you do?* or *Glad to meet you.*

Practice

a. Model the dialog with a student, using the read and look up technique. Then switch parts and model again.
b. Students choose partners and practice the dialog taking first one part and then the other. They should use real information about themselves. Walk around the class, making appropriate suggestions and corrections.

LISTEN TO THIS

This section consists of three short conversations. Have students read the instructions in their books and look at what they will be listening for. Remind them that they don't need to understand every word, just enough to get the necessary information. If they like, they can work on unfamiliar vocabulary items later.

1. For each conversation
   a. Play the tape or read the conversation the first time. Allow students enough time to take notes.
   b. Play or read the conversation a second time, and maybe even a third, giving students the time they need to get any information they missed.
   c. Have students check their answers with each other in small groups.
   d. Write the answers on the board.
   e. At this point, you may want to give students the opportunity to see in print what they've been listening to. Have them turn to the tape-script, at the back of their books, as you replay or read the conversation again.

Answers:

Conversation 1:
Thomas Bradley, a car salesman
Ted Nugent, American Airlines Personnel Department

Conversation 2:
Bill Peters, an engineer for Boeing
Susan Jackson, a medical student at UCLA

Conversation 3:
Bob Evans, a history teacher
Jim Taylor, an accountant for General Motors
(vocabulary: *accountant* – a person who keeps the financial records of a company)

2. From a conversation, native speakers can usually guess the setting, the roles of the speakers and the tone. Students can begin to develop this same ability. Ask:
   a. *Where do the conversations take place?*
   Answers:
   Conversation 1:
   at a business meeting

   Conversation 2:
   The answer is not stated, but since the man offers to buy Susan a drink, it is probably a bar.

   Conversation 3:
   at a party

b. *Which situation do you expect to be more formal than the others?*
   Answer:
   Conversation 1

c. *What words or phrases can you find in each of the conversations which helped you guess the setting and tone?*
   Answers:
   Conversation 1:
   Let me introduce myself.
   How do you do?
   Yes, that's right.

   Conversation 2:
   Yeah, really.
   Is it OK if I sit here?
   Sure. Thanks.

   Conversation 3:
   Sure is.
   Yeah.

IF YOU HAVE TIME ...

Here are some suggestions for other informal situations in which people might introduce themselves to each other. Write each situation on a card or slip of paper. Do not tell the class what the situations are. Have each pair of students take one card. Then have them invent a role-play based on the situation described on their card. Have some or all of the pairs present their role-plays to the class and let the others guess what the situation is. You may need to help the students with vocabulary. Tell them to ask you for words they may need.

1. Two people are at a park watching as their children play. They have seen each other there before, but they have never spoken to each other.
2. Two people are sitting in the waiting room at a dentist's office.
3. One person is sitting alone at a table in the university/company cafeteria. There are no more empty tables. Another person asks to sit down.
4. One person has just attended a lecture given by the other. She/he has an opportunity to talk with the lecturer.
5. You drop by to see a friend, but the door is answered by the friend's sister/brother whom you've never met. Your friend is not home.

UNIT 2

We'll have to fill out some forms

Setting the Scene

Have students look at the photograph on the first page of Unit 2 while covering the conversation. To prepare them for the opening conversation, ask questions about bank accounts: *What kinds of bank accounts can you open? What are the differences between them? Is it difficult to open a bank account? How do you do it? What kinds of questions do they ask you at the bank?*

Vocabulary

Introduce these words now or after students hear the conversation once.

savings account: There are two main kinds of bank accounts in the U.S. People use *savings accounts* to save their money and *checking accounts* to spend it. In a *savings account*, the money you deposit earns interest (usually about 5%). So, for example, if you deposit $100 into a savings account and leave it there for one year, you will have $105 at the end of the year. In contrast, a *checking account* earns no interest; in fact, in some banks you have to pay a monthly service charge. However, you can use the money in the account to write personal checks, and most people in the U.S. like to pay for things this way.

zip code: The U.S. Postal Service uses a system of five numbers to indicate specific areas within each city. This number is used in addresses and appears to the right of the state. For example:
   James Simpson
   420 W. 46th St.
   New York, N.Y. 10036

Listening

1. Play the tape or read the conversation at normal speed.
2. Have students prepare answer sheets. (Items a–g)
3. Write these questions on the board.
   a. What type of bank account does the man want to open? (*savings*)
   b. What is the man's name? (*John Paine*)
   c. What is his address? (*2418 Greystone Road, Chicago*)
   d. What is his zip code? (*60602*)
   e. What is his telephone number? (*364-9758*)
   f. What is his occupation? (*salesman*)
   g. Where does he work? (*IBM*)
4. Follow steps 4–12 outlined in the Introduction.

GIVE IT A TRY

Note: Throughout this section much of the language used is specific to filling out forms. Compare the questions and answers used in this unit to those in Unit 1. This will help students see how similar language functions are expressed differently in different situations. Also, if students are reluctant to give such personal information as home addresses and telephone numbers, tell them they can make up the information.

1. Names

▶ Could I have your name, please?
▷ It's Paine, John Paine.
▶ And how do you spell your last name?
▷ It's P-A-I-N-E.

Pronunciation: series intonation

Series intonation is used in spelling. That is, the voice rises on each element and then falls at the end.

1. Play the cassette or read the dialog. Then play or say each line and have students repeat.
2. On the board write P-A-I-N-E.
3. Then say *It's P-A-I-N-E*, while pointing to the rises and the final fall.
4. Pointing to the intonation lines on the board have students spell *PAINE*.
5. Now have them spell *JOHN*. They should apply the same series intonation.
6. Finally ask a few students to spell their names in the same way.

Practice 1 and 2

Have students practice the exchange with several other students. As they practice, they should write down the student's names. This helps to develop their skill in listening for specific information by means of an activity which in itself has "real-life" value to the students.

2. Addresses

▶ Where do you live?
▷ I live at 2418 Greystone Road.
▶ Is that in Chicago?

Option 1
▷ Yes, that's right.

Option 2
▷ No, it's in River Grove.

Pronunciation: saying building numbers in addresses

Building numbers are divided into groups starting with the last two digits on the right.
2418 twenty-four/eighteen
418 four/eighteen

Exception:
When the second number from the right is 0 the last two numbers are pronounced separately.
105 one/oh/five
2408 twenty-four/oh/eight

1. Play the cassette or read the dialog and let students listen.
2. On the board write: *I live at 2418 Greystone Road.*
3. Point to 2418 and ask a student to read it, or model it yourself.
4. Erase 2418 and write in 418 again asking a student to model it and providing correction if necessary.
5. Proceed in the same way with a few more numbers: 2690, 325, 486, 5990.
6. Then introduce numbers with 0 (105, 2408 etc.) and continue in the same way.
7. Play or read each line in both versions of the dialog and have students repeat.

Of Interest

Students often confuse the prepositions used in addresses.
I live *at* 2418 Greystone Road. (number, street)
     on Greystone Road.   (street)
     in Chicago.   (city)

Draw three concentric circles on the board (something like an archery target). Show that the larger unit requires *in,* the next smallest *on,* and the smallest and most exact *at.*

You may wish to put this on the board as a model and ask several students to supply information with their own addresses.

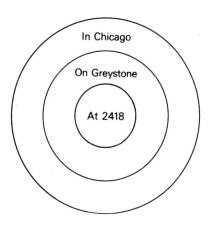

Practice 1 and 2

Have each student practice the exchange with a partner and then move around the room to ask several other students. They should write down the addresses of several classmates.

Practice 3

a. Have each student practice the role-play with a partner and write down the information they get. Allow time for students to change roles.
b. Ask two or three pairs of students to perform the role-play in front of the class. The students who are listening should write down the information as they hear it. They can then check their spelling and accuracy of information with the students who did the role-play.

3. Telephone numbers

▶ What's your telephone number?

Option 1
▷ It's 364-9758 (three, six, four ... nine, seven, five, eight).

Option 2
▷ I don't have a phone.

Pronunciation: saying telephone numbers

When giving telephone numbers, we usually say each number individually with a pause after the first three numbers.
Play or read the dialog. On the board write *It's 364-9758.* Model and have students repeat the phone number. Then write several other phone numbers and have students practice the dialog with them.

Practice 1 and 2

Note: Students may make up numbers if they are uncomfortable giving their real ones.

a. Have each student ask for other students' phone numbers and write the numbers down as they are given.
b. Write the names of some/all of the students on the board and ask the class to call out the telephone numbers of other students.

4. Occupations

▶ And what's your occupation?

▷ I'm a salesman.

▶ What's the name of your employer?

▷ (I work for) IBM.

Pronunciation: review of *wh*-question and statement intonation

Use this model to review rising-falling intonation in *Wh*-questions and statements.
    Play or read the dialog once. Write the dialog on the board and indicate the sentence stresses. Ask students to tell you where the voice should rise. Then draw in the intonation contours. Have students read the lines with appropriate intonation.

Of Interest

Point out the difference between the questions used when filling out a form and those used in friendly conversation.

form questions	**conversation**
What's your occupation?	What do you do?
What's the name of your employer?	Where do you work?

Extension

Refer students to the occupations and companies discussed and used in Unit 1. Have students use these or their own if they are employed.

Practice 1 and 2

Have each student ask several others for the information.

Practice 3

A: Can I help you, ma'am?
B: Yes. I'd like to open a savings account.
A: Certainly. Could I have your name?
B: It's _____
A: And where do you live?
B: I live at _____
A: What's your telephone number?
B: It's _____
A: And your occupation?
B: _____
A: And what's the name of your employer?

Give each student enough time to practice the role-play with two other students. Each student should play each role.

Of Interest

Point out to students that *I'd like . . .* means *I would like . . .*, which is a polite way of saying *I want.* Model the pronunciation of these lines and have students repeat. Listen especially for the inclusion of *'d.*

Extension

Have one or two pairs of students perform the role-play in front of the class. The students who are listening should write down the information they hear. The accuracy of the information can then be checked with the students who did the role-play.

5. Asking personal questions more politely

▶ Could I have your name?

Pronunciation: rising intonation for requests

Requests can be pronounced two ways: with rising intonation as shown above or with rising-falling intonation. It usually sounds more polite to use rising intonation.
    Model the above request for the class using rising intonation and have students repeat. Then have them practice the other requests in their book, using the same intonation.

Practice 1

Ask a student one of the questions. Then have that student ask another question of another student. Continue this chain drill around the class.

Practice 2

Have each student practice the role-play with another student. Allow enough time for each student to take both parts. Have each student write down the information as she/he hears it.

6. Calling Information

▶ Directory Assistance. What city please?

▷ Chicago. I'd like to have the telephone number of Mr. John Paine, please.
▶ Yes, ma'am. How do you spell his last name?
▷ It's P-A-I-N-E.
▶ Thank you. And could you tell me his address?
▷ It's 2418 Greystone Road.
▶ The number is 364-9758.
▷ 364-9758. Thank you very much.
▶ You're welcome. Have a good day.

Note: The first two lines of this dialog introduce new language elements; the rest is review.

Pronunciation: answering the telephone

When answering the telephone with their names or positions, people usually use rising-falling-rising intonation.

For example: *Jim Harris, IBM, Columbia University*.

1. Play the tape or read the dialog and let students listen.
2. Replay the first line or read it.
3. Write it on the board and illustrate its rising-falling-rising intonation.
4. Explain that when answering the telephone with our names we use this pattern.
5. Write other examples on the board: *Jim Harris. IBM. Columbia University*.
6. Then make the sound of a telephone ringing, "pick up" the phone, and have students pronounce the names using appropriate intonation.
7. Now practice saying the whole dialog.

Practice 1 and 2

Divide the class into pairs. Each pair reads the original dialog and then role-plays the operator and caller.

Extension

1. Have students practice the dialog using their own names. This can be role-played in front of the class after the practice.
2. Have students practice "answering the phone" using their own name, the name of their school or company. Remind them to use appropriate intonation.

LISTEN TO THIS

This section consists of two conversations.
For each conversation
a. Play the tape or read the conversation the first time. Allow students enough time to take notes.
b. Play or read the conversation a second time, and maybe even a third, giving students time to get any information they missed.
c. Have students check their answers with each other in small groups.
d. Write the answers on the board.
e. At this point, you may want to give students the opportunity to see in print what they've been listening to. Have them turn to the tapescript at the back of their books, as you replay or read the conversation again.

Answers:
Conversation 1:
Donald Eakins
1446 Pine Street, San Francisco
Sales clerk – Liberty House Department Store, furniture department

Conversation 2:
Albrecht Rosenzweig
Businessman
June 17, 1926
Austria
Visiting brother, 238 E. 82nd St., New York, N.Y.

Of Interest

In much of the world dates are given in the order of day-month-year. In the United States, the usual order is month-day-year. When the month is written in words, a comma is used between the day and the year.

IF YOU HAVE TIME . . .

Each of these role-plays has two roles. One person will take the information from the other. The person taking the information should only be given part A. The other person will be given part B.

1. **A:** You are an order clerk at Dugan's Department Store. A customer will call you to place an order. You must get the person's name, address, telephone number, credit card number, and the number of the item being ordered.

   B: You are calling Dugan's Department Store to order a lamp from a catalogue.
   Item Number: FL583
   Your name: Robin Stevens (Mr. or Ms.)
   Address: 154–66 Rivers Road
   Grand Rapids, Michigan
   Telephone: 739-8372
   Credit card number: 807-6733-1063

2. **A:** You are selling subscriptions to *Today's World Magazine*. It costs $17.95 for one year and $35.00 for two years. You will need to find out the subscriber's name, address, credit card number, and length of subscription.

   B: You are ordering a subscription for *Today's World Magazine*.
   Name: Leslie Lewis (Mr. or Ms.)
   Address: 39 Columbia Avenue
   Boston, Massachusetts 02176
   Credit card number: 173-0995-3162

UNIT 3

So, tell me about your family

Setting the Scene

Books closed. Ask students about their families. *How many sisters and brothers do you have? Are they older or younger? Do any of them work? What do they do?* etc.

Vocabulary

Introduce these words now or after students hear the conversation once.

journalist: a person who writes for a newspaper or magazine

dad: informal for father

mom: informal for mother

Listening

1. Have the students turn to the first page of Unit 3 and look at the photograph.
2. Play the tape or read the conversation at normal speed.
3. List the names of Barbara's family members on the board.
   Ellen (*23, married, two children*)
   Janice (*21, college student, computer science*)
   Cindy (*19, high school*)
   dad (*lawyer*)
   mom (*journalist, travel magazine*)
   Tell the students to copy the names on a piece of paper.
4. Follow steps 4–12 outlined in Unit 1.

GIVE IT A TRY

1. Do you have any brothers or sisters?

▶ Do you have any brothers or sisters?

Option 1
▷ Yeah, I've got three sisters but no brothers.

Option 2
▷ No, I'm an only child.

Pronunciation: intonation of *yes-no* questions

Rising intonation is used at the end of *yes-no* questions. The voice begins to rise on the last stressed syllable and continues to rise.

1. Play the cassette or read the dialog.
2. On the board copy the intonation line for the first line:
3. Then, model the line pointing to the intonation contour.
4. Have students repeat.
5. Write the line on the board. Erase brothers and sisters and substitute other words (or have students suggest other words).
6. Have students practice rising intonation with these new sentences.

Of Interest

Do you have . . . ? and *Have you got . . . ?* are interchangeable.

Practice 1

Pair work. Have students switch roles so that each student both asks and answers the questions.

Practice 2

Have each student ask two or three other class members for the information. Then have two or three students tell the class about the family of one partner. For example, _____ *has two brothers, three nephews, and one niece.*

GIVE IT A TRY

2. How old are they?

▶ How old are they?

▷ The oldest (one) is twenty-three. The second oldest is twenty-one, and the youngest is nineteen.

Pronunciation: intonation of clauses in a series

In a series of clauses, each clause ends with a rising tone, except for the last clause, which ends with a rising-falling tone.
1. Play the cassette or read the dialog.
2. On the blackboard draw the intonation lines:

3. Then, model the second speaker's response while pointing to the intonation lines.
4. Have students practice saying these lines.
5. Now substitute the alternative lines in the Student Book – *My oldest sister* and *the other one* and have students practice saying the lines again.
6. Have students practice the entire dialog.

Practice 1 and 2

Pair work. Try to have one male and one female in each pair to take the roles of Tom and Barbara.

Practice 3

Have each student ask two others about their families.

3. What do they do?

▶ And what do they do?

▷ The oldest (one) is married. The second oldest is in college, and the youngest is still in high school.

▶ What about your dad? What does he do?
▷ Oh, he's a lawyer.
▶ And your mom? Does she work too?
▷ Yeah, she's a journalist.

Pronunciation: review of series intonation

This model can be used to review the series intonation presented in the previous exercise.
   Play or read the dialog. Draw attention to the intonation described above. Then have students practice this sentence, using series intonation, and finally the whole dialog.

Practice 1

Pair work.

Practice 2

Have students ask the information of students they have worked with in the previous practice exercises. Later in the unit, they will give all the information to the rest of the class.

4. Are you married?

▶ Are you married?

Option 1

▷ Yes, I am.

▶ What does your wife do?

▷ She's a housewife.

Option 2

▷ No, I'm single.

Pronunciation: review of question and statement intonation

This model can be used to review the two basic final intonation patterns: rising intonation for *yes-no* questions and rising-falling for statements and *Wh-* questions.
   Have students practice all variations of the dialog. Provide models and correction where necessary.

Vocabulary

divorced: a person whose marriage has been legally ended

widowed: a person whose husband/wife has died
   A woman might also say *I'm a widow*.
   A man might also say *I'm a widower*.

Practice

Have students ask the information of students they have worked with in the previous practice exercises.

So, tell me about your family.

5. Do you have any children?

▶ Do you have any children?

Option 1

▷ No, I don't.

Option 2

▷ Yes, I've got three boys.

▶ And how old are they?

▷ The oldest one is ten. The second oldest is eight, and the youngest one is seven.

Pronunciation: general review of intonation

This dialog involves every intonation pattern practiced so far. As an alternative to the usual procedure, you may want to let your students work in small groups. Assign each group the task of figuring out and then presenting to the class the correct intonation for one of the lines. **Note:** the group that gets *And how old are they*? should be told to give the strongest stress to *old*.

Practice 1

Refer students to the pictures in their books. They should switch roles so that they both ask and answer questions. As you monitor students' performance, listen to their intonation and provide help where needed.

Practice 2

Have students ask the information of students they have worked with in previous practice exercises. Encourage them to show each other pictures of their families if available.

Extension

Students can now put together all the information they have learned about their partners in Exercises 1–5. Choose two or three students to tell the rest of the class about their partners or have the rest of the class ask questions about them, using the structures in the exercises.

6. Getting information about someone's family

▶ May I ask how old they are?

▶ Could you tell me what they do?

Pronunciation: review of rising intonation for requests

This model can be used to review rising intonation for requests. Play or read the dialog. Ask students if the voice goes up or up and down at the end of these questions. Then play or read the dialog again to confirm or correct and have students practice saying the lines. See Unit 1 for other suggestions.

> **Of Interest**
>
> Point out the difference between the direct and indirect question forms. The indirect forms are more polite and formal and are especially used in official or business situations where it might not be considered appropriate to ask personal questions directly.
>
> | Direct question | Indirect Question |
> |---|---|
> | How old are they? | May I ask how old they are? |
> | What do they do? | May I ask what they do? |
> | Where does s/he go to school? | May I ask where s/he goes to school? |

Practice 1 and 2

Have the students practice the interview in pairs. Allow enough time for them to switch roles. After the students have practiced, have one or two pairs of students do it in front of the class.

LISTEN TO THIS

This section consists of two conversations.

1. a. Have the students look at the pictures for Conversation 1.
   b. Play or read Conversation 1 the first time. Give students enough time to number the pictures as the conversation proceeds. Do not ask for information.
   c. Play the conversation again. Give the students enough time to finish numbering the pictures.
   d. Have students check their work with each other.
   e. Check the answers to Conversation 1.
   f. If time permits, have students turn to the tapescript at the back of their books and read silently as you play or read the conversation.

2. Before doing Conversation 2, write the following words on the board and go over their meanings:

   survey: a series of questions used to get information from people

   census: offical counting of the population of a country, city, etc.

   annual: happening once a year

   income: salary, wages

   resident: a person living at a particular address, city or state

Follow steps a–f as in Conversation 1.

Answers:
Conversation 1
1. Three
2. One boy and two girls
3. The boy is 17/Bobby's 17.
   The girls are 16 and 14./Linda is 16, Jennie is 14./
   The older girl is 16, the younger one is 14.
4. Jack
5. 66, retired/consulting/goes fishing

Conversation 2
1. female
2. married
3. Housewife
4. none
5. factory worker
6. about $13,500
7. 4
8. boys: 9, 7, and 6/Girls: 4½
9. a. house b. rented
10. six

IF YOU HAVE TIME . . .

1. A friend has invited you over to meet a foreign guest. Your friend leaves the room for a few minutes to make some tea. You start talking with the guest.
2. It is a long holiday weekend and you are going to visit your family. They live in a different city from you, and you are on a train that takes four hours to your stop. You and your seat partner have been chatting. She/He asks about your family.
3. You are a freshman in college and have been assigned a roommate in the dormitory. You ask each other about your families.

UNIT 4

Hurry up.
We're late.

Setting the Scene

Have the students look at the photo on the first page of Unit 4 while covering the conversation. Ask *What's happening?* Accept any logical responses, but pursue any that indicate the wife is waiting for her husband. Ask students about their families. *Is there one person who is usually slower to get ready than the others? What kinds of things make a person late? Do you think, as a general rule, men are more likely to be late than women? Or the other way around?*

Vocabulary

Introduce these words now or after students hear the conversation once. Use the relevant drawings in the student book where helpful.

cuff links: jewelry used on shirt cuffs (You might demonstrate what they are by showing the cuffs of a shirt, pushing imaginary cuff links through and then holding the cuff together. You can also point out the cuff links in the drawing on p. 24 of the Student Book.)

dresser: a piece of bedroom furniture that holds clothes

jewelry box: a box that holds jewelry

Listening

1. Play the tape or read the conversation a first time. Use normal conversation speed.
2. Have students prepare answer sheets. (Items a–e)
3. Write these questions on the board.
   a. Where is Jim?   (*in the bedroom/upstairs*)
   b. Where are his cuff links?   (*on the dresser next to the jewelry box*)
   c. What else can't he find?   (*his watch*)
   d. Where is it?   (*we don't know/not where Susan says*)
   e. How much time is there before the play begins?   (*an hour and fifteen minutes*)
4. Follow steps 4–12 outlined in Unit 1.

Extension

If time permits, you may wish to talk about the following topics with your students:
If you are going to a play or concert in your country, what do you wear? Do people "dress up" for such events? Is there an accepted "dress code" for different occasions? What is it? Does everyone follow it? If not, who does not and why? Etc.

GIVE IT A TRY

1. Asking where things are

▶ Where are my cúff links?

▷ They're on the dresser next to the jéwelry box.

Pronunciation: stress in NOUN NOUN constructions

With NOUN NOUN constructions such as cuff links and jewelry box, stronger stress is usually given to the first word. For example,
cúff links, jéwelry box, níghtgown, báthrobe

1. Play the cassette or read the dialog.
2. On the board write *cuff links* and *jewelry box* and model these phrases.
3. Ask students to identify which word in each is stressed more. Then confirm (or correct) their observation by putting a stress mark (•) over *cuff* and *jewelry*.
4. Write three more examples on the board for students to pronounce. *Nightgown, earrings, bathrobe.*
5. Have students practice the entire dialog including the variations in their book. Listen especially to their use of stress and provide help if needed.

Vocabulary

Students may need to go over the vocabulary words involved in Practice 1 and 2 of the Student Book. Use the drawing on pages 24–5 of their book.
scarf
stockings
nightgown
boots

Practice 1 and 2

Have students prepare for Practice 1 and 2 by looking at the drawing in their books and reviewing the prepositions and articles of clothing depicted there in small groups. Help them to clarify the meaning of these vocabulary words. Model the pronunciation if necessary. Pair students with members of the opposite sex if possible and have them do Practice 1 and 2.

2. Asking where things are – more politely

▶ Do you know where my watch is?

▷ Isn't it in the top drawer on the right?

Pronunciation: review of rising intonation for *yes-no* questions

Follow the usual procedures for teaching intonation or do the following:

1. Write on the board: *Do you know where my watch is?*
2. Then say, how should I say this:

   Do you know where my watch is?

   OR

   Do you know where my watch is?

3. Confirm or correct students' answers, and have them ask the question.
4. Write the second sentence on the board and follow the same procedure.

Of Interest

When asking someone's help in finding something, we often use the more polite from *Do you know where . . . ?* This is especially important when we can't assume that the other person knows where it is.
Point this out to your students. Also, draw their attention to the difference in word order between the direct and indirect question forms.

Direct	Indirect
Where *is* my watch?	Do you know where my watch *is*?
Where *are* my cuff links?	Do you know where my cuff links *are*?

Practice 1

Pair students with members of the opposite sex if possible.

Practice 2

Pair work. After individual pair practice, have one or two pairs perform the dialog for the class using different objects and locations. The rest of the class can look at the picture to be sure the correct location is given.

3. Asking where things are – outside

▶ Excuse me. Do you know where the theater is?

Option 1

▷ Sorry, I don't know.

Option 2

▷ Sure, it's down this street on the right.

Pronunciation: intonation of introductory expressions

Each of the introductory expressions used in these utterances is given rising-falling intonation, thus setting it off as a separate thought.
   Play or read the dialog. Draw attention to the intonation of *Excuse me, Sorry* and *Sure.* Have students practice saying these words and then the whole dialog.

Practice 1 and 2

Pair work. Practice the exchanges with several different places on the map.

Practice 3

Have groups of three or four students exchange the information.

Of Interest

When describing where something is, we often try to relate it to a place the speaker knows by saying, for example, *Do you know where the post office is? Well, the restaurant is right across the street.*

---

4. Telling time

▶ What time is it now?

▷ It's six forty-five.

Pronunciation: review of rising-falling intonation

Use this model and the following exercise to practice rising-falling intonation in *Wh*-questions and statements.

> **Of interest**
>
> There are usually two ways of telling the same time. For example,
> 6:05 = six oh five   *or* five after (past) six
> 6:45 = six forty-five *or* quarter to seven
> 6:15 = six fifteen   *or* quarter after (past) six
> 6:30 = six thirty   *or* half past six
>
> Either form can be used in conversation.

Practice

Ask individual students to give the time on each clock in two different ways.

5. Starting and finishing times

▶ When does the play start?
▷ It starts at eight (o'clock) (sharp).

Pronunciation: sentence stress

As discussed earlier, stress is given to content words (nouns, verbs, adjectives, adverbs) and to *Wh*-question words. Thus, these words are said louder and held longer. The other words (auxiliary verbs, articles, pronouns and prepositions) are generally not stressed. That is, they are said very quickly, and in order to say them fast, speakers usually reduce them, changing their vowel and/or consonant sounds, which makes it difficult for non-native speakers to understand them.

1. Write on the board *When does the play start?* and mark syllables for stress, using • or any other mark your students may be familiar with.
2. Play the cassette or read the dialog.
3. Model the first line again at normal speed, putting stress on the content words and saying *does* and *the* very lightly and rapidly.
4. Have students repeat.
5. Follow the same procedure for the next line *It starts at eight o'clock sharp.*
6. Practice the whole dialog and its variations.

Practice

This can be done as pair work or in a chain drill, with each student answering a question and then asking the next one. Tell students to listen for correct answers.

6. Opening and closing times

▶ Could you (please) tell me when the store opens?

Pronunciation: review of sentence stress

This model and the alternative in the student book can be used to practice applying the rules for sentence stress presented in the last section.

> **Of Interest**
>
> We usually use the indirect question form when asking for information over the phone.

Practice

Pair work. After the students have practiced the dialog, have one or two pairs perform the dialog.

LISTEN TO THIS

This section consists of three parts. For each part,
a. Have students look at their books so they know what to listen for.
b. Play or read the conversation the first time. Give students enough time to fill in as much information as they can. Do not ask for the information.
c. Let students listen to the conversation again.
d. Check the answers.
e. Optional:
   Let students read the tapescript at the back of their books, as you replay or reread the conversation.

Answers:

1.
a. the TV guide – on the table next to the sofa
b. the strawberry jam – on the top shelf of the refrigerator
c. the aspirin – in the purse on the dresser in the bedroom
d. the sales report – in the file
e. the paperback bestsellers – on the middle shelf to the left of the entrance/the Harold Robbins books – on the right-hand side (of the shelf)

2.

Have students check their answers in small groups while you circulate to answer questions they may have.

3.
a. 10:00–7:00
b. 4:30 – 6:30
c. 8:15 – 10:00 (approximately)
d. 12:45 – 2:00

IF YOU HAVE TIME . . .

Divide the class into groups of five or six. Have each student put one small personal item (a pen, a ring, a key, etc.) near the others on a flat surface. Let the students look at the placement of the items for a minute or so. Then have them cover the items (using a sheet of paper, a handkerchief, a scarf, etc.). Have each student ask another where his/her belonging is. Encourage them to use different forms in asking and answering the questions.

Variations UNIT 5 Variations

1.

a. Have students look at the pictures in the book while they cover the accompanying dialog with a piece of paper. Ask questions such as *Where does the conversation take place? Who are the people? How old are they?* etc.
b. Ask students: *How would you start a conversation in this situation? What would you ask the other person? What kinds of answers might you expect to hear?*
c. Have the students make two columns on a piece of paper.
Have them head one column *Amy* and the other *Bob*. Read the conversation and have half the class fill in information under *Amy* and the other half fill in information under *Bob*. Read the conversation a second time and give students time to add more information to their lists. Have students check their answers with each other. Write the columns on the board and ask students to contribute information.

Possible answers:

Amy	Bob
going to San Francisco	going to San Francisco
parents live in S.F.	family lives in Chicago
one sister	two brothers and a sister
studies at UCLA	studies at UCLA
studies music	studies (any subject)

d. Have the students look at the conversation in their books while you read it. When you come to a blank in the conversation, ask students to give possible alternatives. Here are some:
Bob: Thanks. Nice day *isn't it?*
Amy: Yeah, *really./Yes, it is./Yes, it really is./Yes.*
Bob: Are you *going/traveling* to San Francisco?
Amy: Yeah, *I go to* UCLA.
Bob: ... What *are you studying/are you majoring in?*
Amy: ... What *about you/are you studying?*
Bob: I'm *in the Business School/History Department/the Law School.* Bob Andrews, by *the way.*
Amy: Hi, *I'm/my name's* Amy.
e. Pick out the cue words from each question and answer, and write them on the board. Students may make suggestions.

For example,
B: seat/taken/?
A: No
B: Nice day/?
A: Yes
B: you/San Francisco?
etc.

f. When all the cues are on the board, have the students close their books and work in pairs to try to reconstruct the conversation. (It is not necessary for the reconstructed conversation to be exactly the same as the original. Accept possibilities which are grammatically and situationally correct.) Have them try it orally, referring to the cues on the board when necessary. Then they may write it, and work in small groups to make any necessary corrections. Walk around, providing help as needed.

2.

a. Have the students fill out the form in the book with a pencil.
b. Have the students look at the partial dialog between the two people. Ask for suggestions for appropriate questions. Ask them what type of situation it is (a "form-filling" situation) and what types of questions they would expect to ask and answer. As the suggestions are being given, write cues for each question on the board. For example, *Name, Address.* Ask for ways in which the questions and answers would be given. Practice a few of the more difficult ones. For example, *And what's the name of your employer?*
c. Choose a group of students to come to the front of the class and sit in chairs facing the rest of the class. They will be the ones who take the telephone orders. One at a time they will take the orders from other members of the class. They should write down the information as they hear it. When they have finished getting the information, they should check it by saying, *Now let me see if I have all the information correct. Your name is _____. Your address is _____.* etc. The caller agrees with or corrects the information.

3.

a. Have the students look at the dialog in their books as you read it. Do not fill in the blanks yet. Give the students a chance to get the idea of the entire conversation. After you read the dialog, ask where the conversation takes place, why the people are there, and if they know each other.
b. Have students give suggestions for the blanks in the conversation. Keep in mind the appropriateness of the language for this type of situation. As you accept appropriate forms, write cue words for the conversation on the board. When you have finished, have the students close their books and make appropriate questions and answers from the cues on the board.

c. Then divide the class into pairs and have them reconstruct a conversation based on the cues, this time using information about themselves. It is not necessary for them to write down the new conversation. Have two pairs of students do their dialog for the class. The other class members can comment on appropriateness of language and grammar.

4.

a. Have the students look at the flight chart and at the dialog. Model the exchange, with you acting as the person giving the information.
b. Have several students come to the front of the room and sit in seats facing the rest of the class. These people will act as airline personnel. Have other students call the airline personnel and ask for information on one destination. Without looking at the chart, they should write down the information they hear from the airline personnel. They should then check their information by saying, *Let me check this. That's* (name of airline) *leaving at* _____ *and arriving at* _____. The airline personnel will agree with or correct the information.

Extension

If train or bus schedules are available from the main terminal or station in your city, hand out three or four of them to students who will then act as information personnel. Other students will call and ask about trains or buses for different cities. Follow the same procedure as in Step 2 above.

5.

a. Have students look at the picture which accompanies this exercise. Go over any unknown vocabulary words.
b. Model the dialog with a few of the items in the picture.
c. Divide the class into pairs and give them about 5 minutes to practice asking about the items in the picture. As you circulate, pay attention to correct use of singular and plural for count and non-count items.
d. Have members of the class ask other members (not from their pair work) about items in the picture. After the answers are given, ask other students if the location was correct.

Extension

Divide the class into 2 or more teams. Have students close their books and have each try to remember the items in the illustration and their location. Allow each team about 5 minutes to prepare notes and select a speaker who will tell the class what they remember seeing. If you wish, you can give points using this scoring system:
1 point for each item
1 point for each correct location
1 point for correct use of grammar

LISTEN TO THIS

1. Prepare the students for the "contest" by asking if they have ever seen a quiz show. If they haven't, explain that it is a show in which *contestants* are asked general knowledge questions and get points for correct answers. The person with the most points wins a prize. If they have seen some quiz programs, ask what types of questions are asked, what areas are generally covered, and what types of prizes are given.

2. If you wish to have pair work and then a class activity
   a. Have students close their books and then give them an example of the three types of questions by asking:
      • *What's the capital of Columbia?* (*Bogotá*)
      • *Can you spell that?* (*B-O-G-O-T-A*)
      • *Where is the White House?* (*Washington, D.C., the U.S.*)
      Hold up a picture of a well known person and ask
      • *Who's this?* (*It's* _____.)
      • *What's his/her nationality?* (*She/he's* _____.)
      • *What does she/he do?* (*She/he's a* _____.)
   b. Divide the class into pairs, assign the parts of contestant and host in each pair. Then have them open their books and immediately cover the part used by other person. Then give the students enough time to do all three sections of the quiz. Have them switch roles for each section. Then proceed to the activity described in the next step.

3. If you wish to have only a class activity
   a. With the students' books closed, give examples of the three categories of questions. Choose one person who will act as host and five students to act as contestants. Only the host will need a book until the contestants have to look at the pictures of famous people.

b. Have the contestants line up on one side of the room and have the host stand on the other side. The host will ask the questions one at a time. The contestants raise their hands when they know the answer. On the board list the names of contestants and give points for correct answers. Each answer will be worth two points. With the capitals of countries, give one point for knowing the correct country and one point for correct spelling. For famous places, give one point for the correct country and one point for the correct city. For famous people, give one point for correct nationality and one point for correct occupation.

c. The host should ask all the questions in the first category (capitals) before he/she moves to the next category (famous places). For famous people, have the contestants open their books, cover the answers immediately, and number the pictures in pencil. The host will choose a number at random and say *Who is the person in picture number _____?*

d. Place student points on the board. When the game is finished, the host declares the winner and the prize.

UNIT 6

Are you doing anything tonight?

Setting the scene

Have students look at the picture on the first page of Unit 7 while covering the conversation. Tell them that the names of the two people are Michael and Susan. Michael is calling Susan to ask her for a date. Ask students about dating habits in their country. *Does the man always call the woman? How many days before a date is it necessary to ask someone out? Does the man go to the woman's house to pick her up? How old are people when they begin to date?*

Listening

1. Play the tape or read the conversation at normal speed.
2. Have students prepare answer sheets. (a–d)
3. Write these questions on the board.
   a. When does Michael want to see Susan? (*Saturday/Saturday night*)
   b. Where are they going to go first? (*for a pizza*)
   c. Where are they going to go after that? (*to a new disco*)
   d. What time is Michael going to pick up Susan? (*at 7:00*)
4. Follow steps 4–12 outlined in Unit 1.

GIVE IT A TRY

1. Informal invitations: accepting

▶ Do you feel like going to that new disco Saturday?

▷ Oh, that's a terrific idea.

Pronunciation: review of question and statement intonation

This model can be used to review rising intonation for *yes-no* questions and rising-falling intonation for statements.

Of Interest

Do you feel like...? What about...? and *How about...?* all mean *Do you want to...?* in this context. They are all followed by the *-ing* form of the verb.

Practice

Pair work with male/female pairs if possible. As you circulate be sure that students are making the necessary pronoun changes.

2. Informal invitations: declining

▶ Do you want to have lunch together tomorrow?

▷ Gee, I'm really sorry, I can't. I have to meet a friend.

Pronunciation: blending of *want to* and *have to*

In informal spoken English, Americans frequently blend words together: *want to* sounds like /wanna/; *have to* sounds like /hafta/.

1. Write *want to* and *have to*.
2. Play or read the model pointing to the words on the board.
3. Ask students to tell you how they sounded.
4. Write /wanna/ /hafta/ on the board and have students practice saying these blended forms. Explain that native speakers use these forms in rapid speech. Knowing this will help your students understand spoken English. It is not necessary for them to use these forms in their own speech.
5. Model the complete sentences and have students practice saying them.
6. *Got to* is used in the alternative sentence. Write it on the board. Ask students how they think it sounds in rapid speech /godda/. Then practice the alternative sentences.

Practice

Pair work with male/female pairs if possible.

3. Beginning an invitation

▶ Say, are you doing anything Saturday night?

Option 1

▷ No, nothing special. Why?

▶ Well, what about going to a party?

▷ Oh, that's a great idea.

Option 2
▷ I'm meeting a friend. Why?
▶ Oh, I was going to invite you to a party.
▷ Gee, I'm really sorry. I can't go.

Pronunciation: special intonation

Note the intonation of *No*. The voice rises, as if to ask the speaker why he asked the question.

Of Interest
a. *Say* is similar to *By the way* in Unit 1. It is used to introduce an idea or change the topic of conversation.
b. Questions such as *Are you busy Saturday night?* or *Are you doing anything Saturday night?* are common lead-ins to asking someone for a date.

Practice 1 and 2

Male/female pairs are best for these exercises.

Extension

After the pairs practice individually, have a few pairs of students perform the dialog for the class.
   Ask other class members to recall the time, proposed place, and reason for refusing.

4. Suggesting another time

▶ Gee, I'm really sorry. I can't make it.

Option 1
▷ OK. Maybe we can do it some other time then.
▶ Yes, I'd really like to.

Option 2
▷ Well, how about Friday, then?
▶ Great!

Pronunciation: stressed and reduced forms of *can* and *can't*

Although auxiliaries are generally not stressed, when they are negative, they do receive stress. Note the contrast between *I can't make it* in the first line, where *can* is emphasized, and ... *we can do it* in the second line, where *can*, not stressed, is said very quickly and sounds like /kin/.

1. Draw students' attention to the reduced pronunciation of *can* in contrast to *can't*, using any of the techniques presented in previous sections.
2. Play or read the model and have students repeat.
3. As an option, you might want to give students practice in discriminating between pairs like *I can go* vs. *I can't go*; *I can type* vs. *I can't type*, etc.
4. Model and practice the alternative sentences in the student book.

Practice 1 and 2

Pair work with male/female pairs if possible.

5. Setting the time and place

▶ Where do you want to meet?
▷ Why don't we meet at Shakey's.
▶ Great. What time?
▷ Is seven o'clock OK?
▶ Fine.

This exercise may be done as a chain drill.

Pronunciation: rhythm

English is a stress-timed language. This means that the stresses occur at fairly regular intervals. The sentences in the above model provide a good example of the regular "beat" created by the pattern of stressed and unstressed syllables.

1. Write the first two sentences on the board.
2. Play or read the model, while rhythmically tapping the stressed syllables.
3. Have students say the lines while you tap out the rhythm.
4. Continue with the rest of the dialog.

Practice

Male/female pair work is best for this exercise.

6. More formal invitations: accepting and declining

▶ I was wondering if you'd like to go skiing this weekend?

Option 1
▷ Oh, yes. I'd love to.

Option 2
▷ Oh, I'd love to, but I don't think I can.

Pronunciation: auxiliaries in terminal position

When auxiliaries are the last words in an utterance, they are stressed. To teach this concept, contrast *can* in different positions: *I don't think I can.* vs. *I don't think I can go.* Play or read the dialog and variations and have students practice saying each line.

Of Interest

Would you like to ...? and *I was wondering if you'd like to ...?* are both polite forms used in place of *Do you want to ...?*

Practice 1 and 2
Pair work with male/female pairs if possible.

Extension
Have several pairs of students perform the role-play for the class.

7. Setting another time: more formally

▶ I'm afraid I can't.

Option 1
▷ Well, perhaps we can do it another time then.
▶ Yes, let's.

Option 2
▷ Well, could you make it next week?
▶ Oh. That would be fine.

Pronunciation: blending of *could you*

In rapid speech, *you* is often reduced to *yuh* and *could you* is often blended so that it sounds like /cu-juh/. Use the blackboard to teach this blended form, useful especially for listening. Then model and practice the dialog with its variation.

Practice 1 and 2
Students may use the invitations in Practice 6 or make up their own invitations.

8. Setting the time and place: more formally

▶ Where would you like to meet?
▷ Should we meet at the station?
▶ All right.
▷ What time should we meet?
▷ Would seven be all right?
▶ Fine.

Pronunciation: blending of *would you*

Similar to *could you* in the preceding model, *would you* in rapid speech is often blended and sounds like /wu-juh/. Follow the same procedure as in the preceding section.

Practice 1 and 2
Students can invite their partners to go to dinner or do any other activity. They set their own time and place. If tape recorders are available, have several students practice their dialogs with the recorder. Then play back the tape and listen for pronunciation *or* have other students listen to the tape and restate the invitation.

LISTEN TO THIS

This section consists of two conversations.

1. Dick and Cathy
   a. Have students read the instructions in their books and look at what they will be listening for.
   b. Optional
      If you'd like to ask more questions, write these on the board and have students prepare an answer sheet (items 1–4).
      1) Where did they meet? (*at a party*)
      2) Why can't she go on the first date he suggests? (*She has to work*)
      3) What are they going to do first? (*have dinner*)
      4) What is her address? (*761 Dearfield Drive*)
   c. Play the tape or read the conversation the first time. Allow students enough time to take notes.
   d. Play the tape or read the conversation a second time, and maybe even a third, giving students

time to get any information they missed.
   e. Have students check their answers with each other in small groups.
   f. Check their answers, using any of the procedures suggested in Unit 1.

2. Marge and Ted
   a. Have students read the instructions in their books and look at the multiple choice answers that they will choose from.
   b. Follow procedures c–f as in Conversation 1.

Answers:

1) c
2) b
3) b
4) c

IF YOU HAVE TIME ...

Have students create short dialogs for the following situation, reminding students to consider the relationship between the two people when choosing their language. Assign half of the students the role of invitation giver, telling them: *You have just received an invitation for two to attend the grand opening of an elegant French restaurant. You are going to ask your partner to go with you. Your partner is ...* Assign a role to each of the other students and tell them whether to accept or turn down the invitation. Tell the invitation giver the other person's role. DO NOT tell him/her whether the invitation will be accepted or not. Have one pair of students model a dialog in which the invitation is accepted and another pair do one in which it is refused. As time permits, after the students have practiced in pairs, have them perform the role-play for the class. Comment on language appropriately used.

The invited person is the inviting person's:
a) roommate.
b) girlfriend/boyfriend
c) a classmate they've been wanting to get to know better
d) boss
e) teacher
f) co-worker
g) old friend s/he hasn't seen for several months
h) neighbor
i) business acquaintance from another company

UNIT 7

Which way is the post office?

Setting the Scene

Prepare students for this unit, and find out how well they can give directions by asking questions about nearby buildings. For example, ask *How do you get from here to (a restaurant)?* Ask for other well-known places such as the school cafeteria, a nearby bus stop, etc.

Vocabulary

A simple diagram on the blackboard can be used to illustrate the meaning of *street, corner* and *block*.

For example:

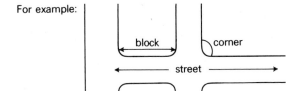

Listening

1. Play or read the conversation the first time.
2. Have students copy the above map on a piece of paper, marking the starting place with an *X* as shown.
3. As they listen to the conversation again, they should follow the directions by drawing a line from the *X* to the post office.

GIVE IT A TRY

1. Asking directions: responding negatively

▶ Excuse me. Which way is the post office?

▷ The post office? Sorry, I'm not sure.

▶ Well, thanks anyway.

Pronunciation: intonation for politeness

Note the intonation of the first line. Instead of using the intonation for *Wh* questions, the speaker uses a rising tone on the *Wh* word and on the last stressed syllable to convey special politeness. The rises in women's voices tend to be higher than those in men's.

Use any of the techniques discussed in Unit 1 to present this intonation pattern. Then have students practice the model above as well as the variation in their books using very "polite" intonation: *How do you get to the post office?*

Practice

Have the students do this practice in a chain drill. They can ask for directions to any place they wish to. One way to have them practice all the variations presented in their books is to require that each student use a different form than the one immediately preceeding him/her.

2. Asking more politely: responding negatively

▶ Excuse me. Would you know how to get to the post office from here?

▷ Sorry, I'm not sure where it is.

▶ Well, thanks anyway.

Pronunciation: review of auxiliaries in terminal position

As seen earlier with the word *can,* when an auxiliary comes at the end of an utterance it is not reduced. In the above model, the auxiliary *is* receives sentence stress. Draw attention to the stress and intonation of *Sorry, I'm not sure where it is* using any of the techniques presented earlier. Then model and have students practice each line of the dialog and its variations.

Practice 1 and 2

Pair work.

3. Asking more politely: responding positively

▶ Excuse me. Could you tell me where the post office is?

▷ Uh, let me see now. It's down this street about two blocks.

▶ Thanks a lot.
▷ You're (very) welcome.

Pronunciation: special intonation

The intonation used in *Let me see now* shows that the speaker is "buying time" while trying to think of something.
1. Play or read the dialog.
2. Draw attention to the new intonation pattern and have students practice it with both sets of words.
3. Then model and have students practice each line of the complete dialog.

4. Giving simple directions

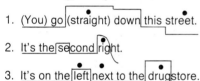

1. (You) go (straight) down this street.
2. It's the second right.
3. It's on the left next to the drugstore.

Pronunciation: review of stress, rhythm and intonation

Use these directions and the variations in their books to help students develop fluency and speed. Tapping out the stresses will help them to keep up the rhythm.

Vocabulary

The expressions *just past* and *just before* mean *immediately past* or *before*.

Practice 1 and 2

Model the role-play with a student. Divide students into pairs for the exercises and, as you circulate, be available to students for any help they may need in giving directions.

Practice 3

Have each student look at the map and choose one building. S/he may ask directions from any other student in the class. If that student doesn't know the location, the answer may be given by any student who does.

5. Giving longer directions (1)

▶ Go (straight) down this street to the end of the block.
▶ It's on the corner on your left.
▶ It's in the middle of the block on your left.

Pronunciation: unstressed words

As pointed out in Unit 4, stress is generally given to content words and not to articles, prepositions, auxiliary verbs and pronouns. These unstressed words are said very lightly and quickly, which is important for the rhythm of English. In rapid speech, they are often reduced so that they are very hard for non-native speakers to understand.

1. Play or read these three lines.
2. To convey the idea of "unstressing" words, write the sentences on the board and draw a line through the words which are not stressed: *It's on the corner on your left.*
3. Model and have students practice the directions given here and the variations in their books.

> **Of Interest**
>
> In the expression *Go straight down this street* the word "straight" means *without turning*. It is used for emphasis and may be omitted.

Practice 1–4

Model one of the directions for the students.
These practice exercises may be done as pair work or as a class exercise. If done as a class exercise, one student gives the directions while the other students look at the map.

6. Giving longer directions (2)

▶ You go down this street for two blocks until you come to the high school. Make a left and go two blocks more. Cross the street, and it's at the end of the block just past Grodin's Men's Shop.

Pronunciation: intonation in a series of directions

Note the frequent rises in pitch which help to break up a long stream of speech and indicate to the listener that there is more to come.
   Play or read the model. Draw attention to the intonation using the blackboard and/or gestures as you replay or reread the lines. Read and have students repeat a sentence at a time and then the whole sequence.

Practice

Pair work. Have each student give directions for two or three of the buildings.

Extension

Have each student silently choose a starting and finishing point on the map. Give them time to figure out the correct directions. Each student will say, for example, *You are in front of the movie theater. Walk north for two blocks. Turn left. Walk two more blocks. The building is in the middle of the block. Which building is it?* The other students look at their maps and identify the building.

7. Confirming and correcting

Option 1

▶ I see. Straight to the corner.

▷ That's right.

Option 2

▶ Left until I come to the end of the block and then right.

▷ No, you turn right and then left.

Pronunciation: special intonation

When given the intonation shown here, *I see* means, *Now I see*, or *Now I understand*.
   Play or read the first conversation. Draw attention to the intonation of *I see*. Read and have students repeat each line. Then play or read the second conversation and have students practice it, working on speed and fluency.

Practice 1 and 2

Pair work. The students may use the buildings in the previous exercise as suggested, or they may choose new places on the map.

Extension: telephone

Think of a nearby building or place of interest and give the directions to a student. Have him/her confirm the directions and then tell the next student, who will, in turn, confirm the directions. The students who are listening may comment on the clarity of the directions given. If the directions are not clear, take suggestions from the class.

LISTEN TO THIS

In this section students will hear three different sets of directions which they will have to follow on the map in their books.
For each conversation:

a. Have students look at their books and be ready to mark the route lightly with pencil in their books.
b. Play the tape or read the directions a first time. Do not check students' work yet.
c. Play the tape or read the directions a second time, and if necessary, a third time.
d. Have students check their maps with others in small groups to see if everyone has drawn the same route.
e. Check each group to see that they have traced the route correctly.
f. **Optional**
   Have students turn to the tapescript, at the back of their books, as you replay or reread the conversations.

Which way is the post office?

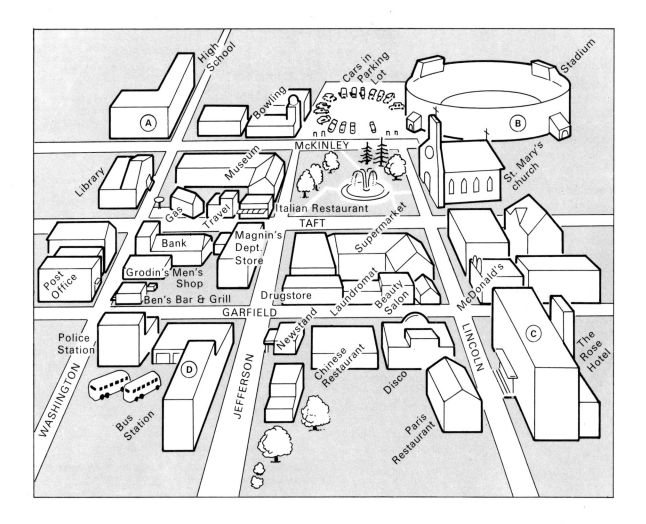

IF YOU HAVE TIME...

This might be a good time to introduce the terms for points of the compass. Those which are most useful for the average person are shown below.

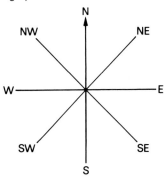

In the compass the various letters have the following meanings:

N – north	S – south
NE – northeast	SW – southwest
E – east	W – west
SE – southeast	NW – northwest

With this vocabulary, students can now describe where various geographical features are located in relation to each other. You may use maps of real places for practice of questions and answers. If possible, have students ask each other about famous places or cities in their own countries. For instance, *Where is Kobe*? Possible answers are: *It's southwest of Tokyo. It's in southwestern Japan. It's not too far from Kyoto. It's just southwest of Kyoto.*

UNIT 8

Do you like jazz?

Setting the Scene

Write the word *jazz* on the board. If possible, have a jazz recording playing as students enter the room, or play the beginning of the tape for this unit. Ask *Do you know what kind of music this is? What kind of music do you like? Who are some of your favorite singers/ groups/composers? Is there any music you don't like?*

Vocabulary

Introduce these words now or after students hear the conversation once.

fusion
Dixieland } styles of jazz

can't stand: strongly dislike (informal)

pushy: very aggressive

I'm not really crazy about it: an informal way of saying *I don't like it very much*

Listening

1. Play the tape or read the conversation at normal speed.
2. Have students prepare answer sheets. (Items a–d).
3. Write these questions on the board.
   a. What kind of jazz does Cathy like best? (*fusion*)
   b. Does she like Dixieland? (*yes/somewhat/a little*)
   c. Does she prefer concerts, records, or radio? Why? (*records/she doesn't like pushy crowds.*)
   d. Does Dick like concerts? Why/why not? (*Probably not much/for the same reason as Cathy.*)
4. Follow steps 4–12, as outlined in Unit 1.

GIVE IT A TRY

1. Likes and dislikes (1)

▶ Do you like jazz?

▷ Oh yes, I love it.

Pronunciation: review of question and statement intonation

Use this dialog to review the rising intonation of yes-no questions and the rising-falling intonation of statements.

Of Interest

The verbs like and love are followed by either the *-ing* form or the infinitive form of a verb. For example, *I like to listen to jazz* or *I like listening to jazz*.

Practice

Pair work or class activity. If done as a class activity, ask any student about one of the items and why s/he likes or dislikes it. Ask other students if they agree.

2. Likes and dislikes (2)

▶ How do you like Dixieland?

Option 1
▷ I'm crazy about it.

Option 2
▷ It's OK.

Option 3
▷ I hate it.

Pronunciation: special intonation

The intonation of *It's OK* shown above gives these words the meaning *It's not bad*. The same words with regular statement intonation would have a different meaning. Play or read the dialogs, drawing attention to the special intonation described here. Then model and have students practice each line, including the variations in their books.

Of Interest

a. Point out to students that *I hate it* and *I can't stand it* are very strong statements in English. A milder form would be *I'm not crazy about it*.
b. In answer to *How do you like ...? It's all right, It's OK* and *It's not bad* show a lack of enthusiasm.

Practice 1

Pair work. Students may use the items in Exercise 1 or they may wish to make up their own items. For example, *How do you like (a currently popular singer or group)?* Ask students to explain their likes or dislikes.

Do you like jazz?

Practice 2 and 3

Pair work. After students have finished comparing their answers with their first partner, they should ask a third student about that student's partner. For example, *How does _____ like tennis?* The third student then replies. While you circulate, listen for correct usage in pronouns and verbs (*How does _____ like tennis? She thinks it's OK*).

3. Agreeing with someone's likes

Option 1

▶ I'm crazy about baseball.

▷ Are you? I am, too.

Option 2

▶ I really like baseball.

▷ Do you? I do, too.

Pronunciation: how stress conveys meaning

There are various ways to read the above sentences. The intonation and stress pattern shown above 1) shows that speakers are talking about a topic which is already known to them and 2) conveys enthusiasm.
    Play or read the dialog. Draw attention to the intonation used. Then model each line and have students practice it, including the variations in their books.

Practice

This exercise may be done as pair work or as a class activity. If done as a class activity, ask several students to ask questions and have other students give the responses.

4. Agreeing with someone's dislikes

Option 1

▶ I don't like hamburgers very much.

▷ No, neither do I.

Option 2

▶ I hate hamburgers.

▷ Yes, so do I.

Pronunciation: how stress conveys meaning

The stress and intonation of these dialogs, like that of the preceding ones, emphasize the speakers' feelings about a topic that is already known to them. Follow the usual procedure for presenting and practicing the dialogs and the variations in the Student Book.

Practice

This exercise may be done as pair work or as a class activity. If done as a class activity, use a random chain drill. (That is, one student asks someone else in the class his/her opinion. This second student answers and then, addressing another student, asks a new question, etc.)

5. Disagreeing with someone's likes

Option 1

▶ I'm crazy about Ella Fitzgerald.

▷ Are you? I'm not.

Option 2

▶ I really like Ella Fitzgerald.

▷ Do you? I don't.

Pronunciation: how stress conveys meaning

There is more than one way to read these lines. The stress and intonation shown above on the first lines indicate that the speaker is introducing the topic (Ella Fitzgerald). This is in contrast to the intonation used in the two preceding models, where the topic was already known. Follow the usual procedure for presenting and practicing the dialogs and their variations.

Of Interest

In some countries it may be considered impolite to show disagreement openly, especially in conversations between people who do not know each other very well. However, it is acceptable in English speaking countries as long as the topic is neutral and the disagreement is conveyed politely.

6. Disagreeing with someone's dislikes

▶ I don't like Elvis Presley very much.

▷ You don't? I like him a lot.

Pronunciation: review of sentence stress and meaning

Note that the first line can be pronounced in different ways, each way reflecting different assumptions, as shown in the preceding models (3, 4, and 5). Play or read the dialog. Model each line or have individual students model them. Then have students practice the dialog and the variations in their books using the same intonation.

Of Interest

I sort of like him and *I kind of like him* are American English equivalents of British *I rather like him.* These expressions show moderate enthusiasm.

Practice

This may be done as pair work or as a class activity. If done as a class activity, have some students ask the questions and other students give appropriate responses.

Vocabulary

Woody Allen: a U.S. actor, director, writer especially known for his humor

Billie Jean King: a famous woman tennis player

7. What kind of ... do you like?

▶ What kind of music do you like?

▷ All kinds, but especially jazz.

Pronunciation: blending of *kind of*

In rapid speech, *kind of* sounds like /kin-da/ or even /kina/.

Play or read the dialog. Draw attention to the blended form of *kind of* (primarily to help students understand native speakers). Ask them to guess how *sort of* and *type of* might sound in rapid speech (/sorta/, /typa/). Model and have students practice each line and the variations, with blending optional.

Practice

Pair work. After students have practiced in pairs, have students compare their preferences and possibly give reasons for them.

Vocabulary

rhythm and blues: a style of jazz that has its roots in Afro-American folk music

mysteries: detective stories such as those by Agatha Christie

romances: stories about romantic love

science fiction: stories about imaginary developments in science, for example: "Star Wars"

non-fiction: any factual writing, including biographies, true adventures, works on science and art, history, etc.

horror movies: frightening movies like *Frankenstein*

football: a popular team sport played in the U.S.

8. Favorites

▶ What's your favorite band?

▷ I like Chuck Mangione best.

Pronunciation: reduced form of *your*

In rapid speech *your* is pronounced /yer/.

Play or read the dialog. Draw attention to the reduced pronunciation of *your* in fast speech to help students understand native speakers. Then have students practice saying each line and the variations in their books.

Practice

Pair work.

Extension

After students have had enough time to finish all the categories, have them compare their answers with other class members.

9. Preferences

▶ Do you like going to concerts?

▷ Sure, they're all right, but I like listening to records better.

Pronunciation: contrastive stress and intonation

The voice rises on *records* as well as on *better* to emphasize the contrast between *records* and *concerts*.
  Play or read the dialog. Draw attention to the intonation of the second sentence. Have students practice the dialog including the variations in their books.

Practice 1
Pair work.

Practice 2
Pair work. Give students enough time to do the exercise and then ask different pairs of students about their work. One student might say *I like jazz, but _____ prefers rock 'n' roll.* Pay particular attention to the use of *s* as in *Toshio prefer<u>s</u> _____*

LISTEN TO THIS

This section consists of two parts.

1.
a. Play the tape or read the conversation the first time. Give students enough time to check the correct box.
b. Play the tape again.
c. Check the answers.

Answers:
a. Agree
b. Agree

2.
a. Have the students look at their books so they know what they will be listening for. You may need to go over the following vocabulary items before the students hear the conversation.
  Fellini: a famous Italian director
  Bergman: a famous Swedish director
  Kurosawa: a famous Japanese director
b. Play the tape or read the conversation the first time and give students time to write as much information as they can.
c. Play the tape or read the conversation again and give students enough time to finish answering the questions.
d. Check the students' answers.

Answers:
a. No
b. Westerns
c. Clint Eastwood
d. (He's the) strong, silent type

IF YOU HAVE TIME...

1. You are trying to "fix up" (arrange a date for) one of your classmates with a friend. The classmate wants to know something about your friend's likes and dislikes.
2. You have invited a friend to dinner. S/he tells you that her/his sister is visiting from out of town. You invite her to come also. You try to find out something about your friend's sister's likes and dislikes in the areas of food, drink, and entertainment.

UNIT 9

And what did you do then?

Setting the Scene

Ask about students' backgrounds. For example, *What city did you grow up in? Where did you go to high school? Have you ever lived in another city? Where? How long did you live there? How old were you when you moved?*

Vocabulary

Introduce these words now or after students have heard the conversation once.

suburb: a small, mostly residential town close to a city Although the plural is used here, *in the suburbs* means in *one* suburb.

Listening

1. Play the tape or read the conversation at normal speed.
2. Have students prepare answer sheets. (Items a–d)
3. Write these questions on the board.
   a. Where was Kevin born? (*Chicago/in Chicago*)
   b. Where did he go to high school? (*Los Angeles/in Los Angeles/Lincoln High School*)
   c. What did he do after high school? (*traveled/went to Europe/lived in Munich*)
   d. How long did he stay there? (*almost two years*)
4. Follow steps 4–12 outlined in Unit 1.

GIVE IT A TRY

1. Talking about personal history

▶ Were you born in Los Angeles?
▷ No, I was born in Chicago.
▶ Did you grow up there?
▷ Yeah, I grew up in the suburbs.
▶ Did you graduate from high school in Chicago?
▷ No, I graduated from Lincoln High.

Pronunciation: blending of *did you*

In rapid speech, *did you* is often pronounced /did-juh/ or /did-ju/.

Play or read the dialog drawing attention to this rapid speech form, which is especially important in understanding native speakers. Then have students practice saying each line.

> **Of Interest**
>
> The above questions can be asked out of real interest in the other person's background. The questions are also asked to carry the conversation along until a point of mutual interest is established.

Practice

Pair work. Use male/female pairs if possible. As you circulate around the room, pay attention to whether the past tense is being used correctly in question and answer forms.

2. Clarifying information

▶ I moved out here when I was fourteen.
▷ So you went to high school here?
▶ Yeah, that's right.
▶ I graduated from Lincoln High.
▷ And then you went to college?
▶ No, not exactly. First I went to Europe.

Pronunciation: intonation questions

In informal conversation rising intonation can be used to change a statement into a question. Follow the usual procedure to teach this point and have students practice the dialog.

> **Of Interest**
>
> The usual question form is *Did you go to high school here?* However, when we assume that the answer is *Yes* we often use the statement form with a rising intonation at the end. The form is used to check that our assumption is correct.

Practice 1

Pair work. Use male/female pairs if possible. As you circulate around the room, check to see that the students are using appropriate intonation.

Practice 2

Pair work. If students have trouble asking questions, you might suggest possibilities such as:
studied hard — got good grades
had lots of friends — were popular
played baseball and volleyball — liked sports
played the violin in high school — liked music

3. Being specific

▶ I lived in Munich for a while.
▷ Did you? And when was that?
▶ That was about eleven years ago.

Pronunciation: reduced form of *for*

In rapid speech *for* is pronounced /fer/. Follow the usual procedure to teach this point and have students practice the dialog, including the variations in their books.

Practice 1, 2 and 3

Pair work. As you circulate around the room, check to see that students are using the words *ago* and *in* correctly.

Practice 4

Pair work. If students have difficulty with information, you might provide cues such as: *begin school, find my first job, join the Boy Scouts, drive my first car, change schools,* etc.

4. Length of time

▶ How long did you stay in Munich?
▷ I stayed there for two years.

Pronunciation: review of *did you*

This can be used to review the blended form of *did you* and to practice stress and intonation. Play or read the dialog and have students practice each line as well as the variations in their books.

> **Of Interest**
>
> The phrase *from* 1973 *to* 1975 can also be *from* 1973 *(un)til* 1975.

Practice

This exercise may be done as pair work or group work. In either case, encourage the students to vary their responses by using different structures in the responses.

5. What next?

▶ And what did you do after leaving Chicago?
▷ Well, then I went to high school in L.A.

Pronunciation: blending of *what did you*

In rapid speech the words *what did you* are often blended to sound like /wu-did-juh/ or even /wud-juh/.
Play or read the dialog. Draw attention to the blended forms of *what did you.* Then model and have students practice each line. Tell them to think of *what did you do* as one word and work for fluency in saying it.

Practice 1 and 2

Pair work. Allow enough time for students to practice both the questions and the answers. As you circulate, check to see if the informal blending of *what did you* is being tried.

Practice 3

Pair work.

Extension

If students have been working with the same partners throughout this unit, they can construct a similar dialog based on the information they have learned about each other.

LISTEN TO THIS

This section consists of two parts. The first is an interview and the second is a college lecture. Follow this procedure for each part.
a. Have students read the instructions in their books and look at what they will be listening for.
b. Preview any necessary vocabulary.

c. Play the tape or read the conversation the first time. Allow students enough time to take notes.
d. Play or read the conversation a second time, and maybe even a third, giving students the time they need to get any information they missed.
e. Have students check their answers with each other in small groups.
f. Write the answers on the board.
g. At this point, you may want to give students the opportunity to see in print what they've been listening to. If so, have them turn to the tapescript at the back of their books, as you replay or read the conversation again.
h. Check the answers.

1.

Answers:
1. False (*ballet dancer*)
2. True
3. True
4. True
5. False (*She went to Europe*)
6. False (*Amsterdam*)
7. False (*1978*)
8. False (*she loves both cities*)
9. False (*a year and a half ago*)
10. False (*in February*)
11. True

Vocabulary
a break: a lucky opportunity
homesick: a feeling of missing one's home
It was just one of those things: it was something unintentional that happened
the Big Apple: a nickname for New York City
curtain: a warning that the performance is about to begin

2.

Answers:
1. 1899
2. doctor
3. in high school (a)
4. (newspaper) reporter
5. no
6. 1925
7. The Sun Also Rises
8. no
9. no
10. The Old Man and the Sea
11. no

Vocabulary
reporter: a person who supplies news to a newspaper, radio or TV.
reject: refuse to accept

IF YOU HAVE TIME . . .

Make up a time line with events and the dates of their occurrence. Use events in your own life or the lives of one or more of the students. Have students use the time line to practice asking and answering questions.

Variations — UNIT 10 — Variations

1. Jigsaw reading: An invitation

a. Have the students read the directions and look at the picture in their books.
b. Divide the class into male/female pairs if possible. Then, starting with Part 1, have the women in the class cover George's part and the men cover Karen's part.
c. Give the students a few minutes to look at their parts. Ask them to number the lines with pencil in the order they think they would be said. At this point they have not seen or heard the other part of the conversation.
d. Have each pair read the lines in the order they think they would be said. Begin with George's first line.
e. At this point, each pair can look at both parts in the book and work together to make any necessary changes in the order of lines.
f. Have students do the same for Part 2.
g. Read the dialog.
h. Have one or two pairs of students role-play the conversation for the class.

2. Making a date

a. Divide the class into male/female pairs if possible. Have student A fill in five specific engagements in the appointment book. Have Student B think of a specific event to which she/he will invite Student A. Then have each pair role-play the parts until they can decide on a mutually acceptable time. As you circulate, notice whether students are using appropriate language. Provide help where needed. If necessary, students can review Unit 6.
b. When all the students have had enough time to role-play the conversation, have students switch partners and roles so that those who received invitations now extend them and those who extended invitations now receive them. After they have reached a mutually acceptable time, ask the other students questions such as *Why couldn't she go out on _____ night? Where did he ask her to go? When will they go?*

3. Finding the way

This activity can be done by groups of three. Two of the students in each group are on their way to the play of their choice when they stop to ask the third student, "the stranger," for directions. (The first pair should not tell the third student their destination before the role-play begins.) The helpful stranger refers to his/her map and gives the directions. While one of the pair repeats the directions to be sure they were understood, the other member of the pair should follow the directions on the map.

As you circulate, provide help where needed. If necessary, students can review Unit 7.

4. The visitors

a. Divide students into pairs. Give them time to read the letter. When they finish reading, they should exchange information without reading it from the book. Encourage students to find common points of interest from the letter.
b. Have the students select several points of interest in their town which would appeal to both Bob and Janet. They may decide where to meet after their separate trips. Have the students give the reasons for making their choices.
c. After the students have worked for some time in pairs, have several pairs compare their ideas or call on several pairs to give their ideas and ask the rest of the class to comment or add suggestions.

5. My favorite: (A Guessing Game)

This game can be played as a whole class activity, or if your class is very large, you can divide the students into groups of ten. In each group one person thinks of a famous person and the others have to guess who it is. Students should ask questions one at a time. Encourage them to begin with questions such as those suggested in their books. As they continue, their questions should become more specific: *Is this person in politics? Did this actor make a film about mountain climbing?* etc. Students may guess the name at any time by asking *Is this person (name)?*

LISTEN TO THIS

Part 1

a. Have the students look at the pictures in the book and try to guess where they are. Ask what they know about the different places. This will familiarize them with their choices.
b. Play the tape the first time. Have the students mark the sequence of pictures with a pencil.
c. Play the tape a second time and give students time to complete the task.
d. Check the sequence of pictures.

Answers:

Extension

Have the students try to reconstruct Mr. Thorndike-Lodge's life by going through the pictures one at a time and adding information they remember from the taped conversation. Do this in chronological order and ask different members of the class to add any information they can.

Part 2

a. Have the students look at the questions in their books.
b. Play the tape a third time. Students should write down the answers as briefly as possible on the piece of paper. Tell them not to worry about grammar or spelling.
c. Play the tape again with pauses, allowing students to correct their answers.
d. Have students check their answers in small groups.
e. Have someone write the answers on the blackboard as a final check.

Answers:
 1. no (Bombay)
 2. father — British; mother — Indian
 3. army officer
 4. England
 5. six
 6. 1945 (when he was 18)
 7. 4 years
 8. Egypt
 9. Indonesia
10. traveling (through Asia by train)

UNIT 11

And what would you like?

Setting the Scene
Have the students look at the picture on the first page of Unit 11. Ask: *What's happening in the picture? What are the people going to order?* As they name foods, write them on the board.

Vocabulary
Introduce these words now or after students hear the conversation once.

chef's salad: a large salad with meat, egg, cheese, lettuce and tomatoes

medium rare: meat cooked so that the inside is pink

rare: meat cooked so that the inside is red

medium: meat cooked to an even color

well-done: meat cooked so there is no redness or pinkness inside

(salad) dressing: A sauce to put over a salad. Some popular dressings in the United States are: Italian (oil, vinegar, herbs and spices including garlic), French (milder than Italian and red in color), and Russian (mayonnaise and ketchup).

Listening
1. Play the tape or read the conversation at normal speed.
2. Have students prepare answer sheets with two columns. Put the name Maria at the top of one column and Helen at the top of the other. Have students write down what each woman orders.
3. Follow steps 4–12 outlined in Unit 1.

Answers:

Maria	Helen
chef's salad	cheeseburger
Russian dressing	french fries
coffee	coffee
	sliced tomatoes

GIVE IT A TRY

1. In a restaurant: expressing wants among friends/family

▶ What are you going to have, Helen?

▷ (I think) I'll have a cheeseburger and french fries.

Pronunciation: blending of *going to*

In rapid speech *going to* sounds like /gonna/. Play or read the dialog. Then follow the usual procedure for drawing attention to the blended form of *going to* and have students practice saying the lines.

> **Of Interest**
>
> There are various ways to express future in English. In the above dialog *having* (present continuous) could be used instead of *going to have*.

Practice 1
This exercise can be done as a chain drill. Ask one student and accept any reply. That student then asks another, and so on around the class.

Practice 2
Pair work. When the students have had enough time to decide on their orders, you might ask several students for their choices.

2. In a restaurant: speaking to a waiter/waitress

▶ What would you like, ma'am?

▷ I'll have the chef's salad, please.

Pronunciation: special use of rising intonation

Rising intonation is usually used for the word *please* at the end of a sentence. Play or read the lines. Then draw attention to the intonation described above and have students practice these lines as well as the alternates in their books.

> **Of Interest**
>
> All of the questions in the model have approximately the same meaning, as do all of the responses. However, the use of *would* and *could* is considered slightly more polite than *will*. The response using *will* is particularly appropriate for use in restaurants.

Practice

Pair work. Give students enough time to decide on their orders. As they role play, have them use different ways of asking for and giving the orders.

3. In a restaurant: specifying wants

▶ What kind of dressing would you like?
▷ I'll have Russian (please).

Pronunciation: blending of *would you*

In rapid speech the words *would* and *you* are frequently blended to sound like /wu-juh/. Play or read the model. Then draw attention to the blended form of *would you* and have students practice saying the lines.

Practice 1

Pair work. Give students enough time to make several selections and to switch roles.

Practice 2

Pair work.

Extension

If time permits, have one student act as the waiter/waitress who takes several orders. The other students should write down the orders they hear.

4. In a restaurant: asking about wants

▶ Would you care for anything to drink?
▷ Do you have any iced tea?

Option 1
▶ I'm afraid we don't.
▷ Well, I'll have coffee, then.

Option 2
▶ Yes, certainly.

Pronunciation: polite intonation

To convey special politeness the voice rises higher than usual in the utterance *Yes, certainly*.
 Play or read the dialog. Then draw attention to the special intonation feature and have students practice using a higher rise in their voices as they say *Yes, certainly*. Practice each line in both dialogs.

Practice

Pair work. Have each student cover the other student's part during this exercise. Then have them switch roles.

5. In a restaurant: asking about other wants

▶ Would you like anything else?

Option 1
▷ No, thank you.

Option 2
▷ Not right now, thank you.

Option 3
▷ Yes. Could you bring me a piece of apple pie?

Pronunciation: review of intonation

Play or read the dialog. Have students work in small groups to decide how each line should be said. Confirm (or correct) their pronunciation. Then have them practice saying both versions of the dialog, working on fluency.

Practice

Pair work.

6. In a restaurant: offering service

▶ Shall I bring your coffee (now)?
▷ Yes, please.

Pronunciation: review of intonation

The intonation used in the preceding section for *No thank you* can be applied to *Yes, please*. Play or read the dialog. Draw attention to the intonation of *Yes, please* and have students practice saying that line and then the entire dialog, including the variations in the student book.

And what would you like?

Practice

Pair work. Encourage students to use different question forms with each repetition.

7. At someone's house for dinner: offering and accepting food

▶ Can I offer you another cup of coffee?
▷ No, thanks. I've had plenty.
▶ Would you like anything else?

Option 1
▷ No, thanks. It was delicious, but I've already eaten too much.

Option 2
▶ Is there anything else I can get you?
▷ Yes, please. Could I have some more turkey?

Pronunciation: stress and intonation

In the sentences indicated above, note that there is strong sentence stress on the words *already* and *else*.
   Play or read Option 1 of the dialog. Draw attention to the stress and intonation in the last sentence. Then have students practice the dialog and the alternatives to sentence 1.
   Do the same for Option 2, drawing attention to the stress on *else*. Model the dialog, including the alternative expressions given in the last sentence. Have students practice the lines.

Practice

Group work. Divide the class into groups of four or five people. One woman will act as hostess and one man will act as host. The others are guests at their house. They continue the role play until all the guests have responded. If time allows, change the roles of host and hostess and continue to practice.

Vocabulary

Students may need to review the following vocabulary items before doing the role play:

helping: a serving of food
turkey: a large bird used for food, traditional for Thanksgiving
stuffing: a combination of ingredients put inside something before it is cooked
cider: a drink made from apples

Of Interest

1. The question *Can I offer you* . . . is rather formal. More informally we might say *Would you like* . . . or *How about* . . .
2. When someone from the U.S. invites you to have something to eat or offers more of something, it is polite to accept the first invitation. They will only sometimes offer more than once. This may be in contrast to cultures where it is considered rude to accept the first time.

LISTEN TO THIS

1.

a. Have the students open their books and look at the menu. Explain any unknown items on the menu.
b. Play the tape or read the conversation the first time and allow students time to fill in as much as they understand.
c. Play or read the conversation the second time and give students time to complete their answers.
d. Check the answers.

Answers:
F: baked salmon, boiled potatoes, asparagus salad with blue cheese dressing, coffee
M: steak, (onion) soup, baked potato, broccoli

2.

Follow the same procedure as in Part 1.

Answers:
whole wheat bread   apples
tomatoes   eggs
lettuce   pork chops

3.

Follow the same procedure as in Part 1.

Answers:

Who is she talking to?	What does she want?
a) a post office clerk	a) six 20 cent stamps, five aerograms, four post cards
b) her son	b) her son to eat fruit
c) telephone operator	c) person-to-person call (to Robert Ritchie)
d) her husband	d) help in putting up the curtains
e) store clerk	e) to exchange a sweater

IF YOU HAVE TIME...

1. You are at a friend's house for dinner. You offer to help set the table.
2. You are driving along a highway when you get a flat tire. You pull over to the side and get out. Another motorist stops and asks if she/he can help.
3. A new person is moving into the apartment across the hall from you. Crates are all over the place. You stop in to see if you can help.
4. You have a serious case of the flu. You won't be able to go to an important class. A friend offers to help you out. (Tell the professor, take notes, deliver your assignment, etc.)

UNIT 12

How have you been?

Setting the Scene

Have the students look at the picture on the first page of Unit 12. Ask *What do you think is happening here?* Accept any logical responses. Then, confirm or explain that the picture shows an accidental meeting of friends. Now ask: *If you accidentally meet a friend you haven't seen for a while, what are some of the things you might talk about?*

Vocabulary

Introduce the following vocabulary items now or after students hear the conversation once.

for ages: for a long time

How's . . . doing?: How is . . . ?

No kidding?: Really? (an expression of surprise)

I have to run: I have to leave because I'm in a hurry

Talk to you later: I'll talk to you soon

Give my love to . . .: Give my regards to . . ./Say hello to . . . for me (Used in informal speech with no romantic connotation.)

Listening

1. Play or read the conversation at normal speed.
2. Have students prepare answer sheets. (Items a–f)
3. Write these questions on the board.
   a. Have Jackie and Diana spoken recently? (*No.*)
   b. What does Ted do for a living? (*Works in an office.*)
   c. What has their friend Rita done? (*Asked for a divorce.*)
   d. When did she do it? (*About two weeks ago.*)
   e. Where is Rita's husband living? (*In a hotel.*)
   f. Why can't Diana stay and talk? (*She's late.*)
4. Follow steps 4–12 outlined in Unit 1.

GIVE IT A TRY

1. Greetings

▶ Jackie!

▷ Diana! I haven't seen you for ages. How've you been?

▶ Just great. And you?

Pronunciation: emphatic intonation

Note the wider range in pitch used in the stressed words in these sentences. Wide ranges in pitch are used generally for emphasis. In this case they show surprise, and enthusiasm. (Women tend to vary their pitch more than men.)

Play or read the dialog. Draw attention to the wide range in pitch. Then have students practice the dialog, including alternative sentences.

Vocabulary

can't complain: pretty good

Practice

This exercise can be done as a class activity. Greet one student, who responds. That student greets any other student in the class. Continue until all students have greeted and responded.

2. Asking about others

▶ And how's Ted doing?

▷ Oh, he's OK.

Pronunciation: special intonation

Point out to students how the voice rises, falls and rises again in *He's OK*. Model and have students practice the dialog, including alternative expressions.

Practice 1

This exercise can be done as a class activity. Ask one student how another student is doing. That student responds and asks any other student.

Practice 2

Pair work. Have students ask about mutual friends or relatives.

3. Gossiping

▶ By the way, have you heard about Rita?

▷ No, what about her?

▶ She's asked for a divorce.

▷ Really! When did that happen?

Pronunciation: sentence stress

Draw attention to the stress on *about* in the second sentence and on *that* in the last one. Model and have students practice the dialog and all of the variations.

Draw attention to the use of the simple past tense in the question *When did that happen?*

Practice

Pair work. Have the students use as many of the responses as possible. As you circulate around the room, check students' stress and intonation.

4. Reacting

Conversation 1

▶ Bob's moved oút.

▷ Oh, that's too bad.

Conversation 2

▶ Jim and Carol have had a baby.

▷ How wonderful!

Pronunciation: stress in two-word verbs

In separable two-word verbs, the stress is placed on the final particle. Point out how this works using a few examples:
Bob's moved oút.
Look it úp.
Put it dówn.
Have students practice the dialogs and their variations.

Practice

Pair work. Have students use as many responses as possible.

5. Ending a conversation (1)

Option 1
▶ I've got to run.

Option 2
▶ I'll call you.

Pronunciation: blending of *got to*

In rapid speech *got to* is often blended to sound like /godda/. Thus, *I have got to go* becomes /I've godda go/. Students may hear Americans reduce the *I've got to* even further to /I godda/. They should be aware of the second reduction but should not practice it.

Play or read the dialog. Draw attention to the blended pronunciation of *got to* and have students practice saying that line and the alternate ones in their book rapidly and rhythmically.

Practice 1

Pair work. Give students enough time to practice several of the exchanges.

Practice 2

Choose one student in the class and do the role-play with him/her. This exercise incorporates many of the exchanges in previous exercises. Allow students enough time to incorporate all of the exchanges naturally. If a tape recorder is available, record some of the exchanges. Then play them back for the entire class to hear. Ask appropriate questions about people and events mentioned in each role-play.

6. Ending a conversation (2)

▶ Well, talk to you later, then. Oh, and give my love to Ted.

▷ I will. So long.

Pronunciation: reduced form of *to*

In rapid speech, *to* is often reduced to /tuh/. Play or read the dialog. Draw attention to this reduced form, and have students practice saying the lines.

Practice 1

Pair work.

Practice 2

Pair work. Have students make up interesting or amusing bits of information about their classmates. Have some of the pairs do their role-plays for the class. Here are a few possibilities.

quit her/his job   won a contest
is getting married/eloped   is going to (<u>country</u>) to study

7. Greeting people — more formally

▶ Hello, Mrs. Johnson. How are you today?

▷ Fine, thank you.

▶ And how is Mr. Johnson?

▷ Oh he's fine, thanks.

How have you been?

Pronunciation: Contrastive stress

Mr. is stressed in the third line to contrast with the earlier use of *Mrs.*

Play or read the dialog. Point out the sentence stress described above and have students practice saying these lines.

Practice

Pair work.

Model the exchange twice and have students repeat. Ask students to point out differences between these more formal greetings and those we use with friends. They should be able to distinguish some of the following points.

Formal		Informal
Hello		
Good morning	vs.	Hi
How are you today?	vs.	How's everything?
		How're things?
Thank you	vs.	Thanks

8. Ending a conversation — more formally

▶ Please excuse me, but I really have to be going.
▷ Yes, of course. It was nice to see you.
▶ It was nice to see you, too. And please give my regards to Mr. Johnson.
▷ I will. Goodbye.

Ask the students to point out differences between the formal and informal endings of a conversation. They should be able to mention:

Formal		Informal
Please excuse me.	vs.	Sorry.
I really have to be going.	vs.	I really have to run.
It was nice to see you.	vs.	Nice seeing you.

Pronunciation: contrastive stress

When the first speaker says *It was nice to see you*, stress is placed on the word *see*. However, when the second speaker repeats the statement, stress is placed on *you* (and *too*, if used).

Play or read the dialog. Ask students to identify the sentence stresses in it. Then have them practice saying the lines.

Practice 1 and 2

Pair work.

LISTEN TO THIS

1.

This section consists of four short conversations. Students have to select an appropriate line to complete each one.
a. Have students read the instructions and look at their choices for completing the first conversation.
b. Play or read the conversation the first time and give the students enough time to check their responses.
c. Ask which choice was correct and why.
d. Follow the same procedure for the remaining conversations.

Answers:
Conversation 1.
b) *I'm sorry to hear that* (a general response to bad news).
The other responses are inappropriate for these reasons:
a) *No kidding* is an informal response to surprising news but does not show that the speaker is sad to hear it.
c) *That's terrific* is an informal response to good news.

Conversation 2.
b) *You don't say* is a response to surprising news, either good or bad.
The other responses are inappropriate for these reasons:
a) *See you* is an informal parting comment.
b) *How terrible* is a response to bad news.

Conversation 3.
c) *Oh, that's too bad* (A response to bad news).
The other responses are inappropriate for these reasons:
a) *Oh, not really* would be an appropriate response to a question such as *Are you doing anything tonight?*
b) *Oh, that's not bad* usually means *That's a good deal*, i.e. a bargain.

Conversation 4.
c) *Oh, I can't complain.* (A positive response to a question such as *How are you?*)
The other responses are inappropriate for these reasons:
a) *Take care* is a parting response.
b) *I've got to run* is a response used to end a conversation.

2.

Part 1

a. Have the students read the directions and look at the pictures in their books. Ask general questions about what is happening in each.
b. Play or read all the conversations once, or let them hear without stopping and then go back to all of the conversations a second time. This time students will write the number of each conversation under the corresponding picture.

Part 2

a. Have the students look at the expressions of time in the book. Go over each of the phrases to be sure that students understand the correct meaning of each.
b. The students have already heard the conversations twice. Tell them that they will now hear each conversation once more. They need only listen for the phrase which tells when the main event happened.
c. Let them hear the conversations again. Stop after each conversation allowing students time to write in their answers.
d. If necessary, play or read the conversation a second time.

Answers:
a) last week/last Friday
b) a couple of weeks ago
c) the day before yesterday
d) last weekend
e) last Thursday

2. Sam telephoned me at midnight.
   a. This is very romantic.
   b. This is an outrageous time to telephone.
   c. You are the last person in the world Sam would phone.
   d. Sam is the last person in the world you would expect to phone.
   e. Sam was supposed to be at your home at seven. He didn't appear.

IF YOU HAVE TIME...

Let students practice using their voices to express different emotions. Give them the sentences one at a time and tell them what emotion to show. Have them read the sentence aloud using their voices to express the given attitude.

1. Lou is taking Carol to the movies Saturday evening.
   a. Show surprise that it's Lou, not another man.
   b. Show anger that he's taking Carol.
   c. Show happiness that Lou and Carol are going together.
   d. Show happiness that they are going to the movies.
   e. Show disappointment that they are going Saturday.

UNIT 13

What did the person look like?

Setting the Scene

Have the students look at the picture on the first page of Unit 13. Ask students to describe the people in the picture in terms of height, weight, color of hair and eyes, and color and type of clothing. If time permits, have them describe one or two class members and let other students guess who is being described.

Vocabulary

Introduce these words now or after students hear the conversation once.

kind of: rather

denim: A heavy cotton material, usually blue. Jeans are made of denim.

vest: a waist-length, sleeveless article of clothing, usually worn over a shirt

pound: abbreviated as *lb.*, 0.45 kilograms

foot: abbreviated as *ft.* or ′, 30 centimeters

inch: abbreviated as *in.* or ″, 2.5 centimeters

Listening

1. Play the tape or read the conversation at normal speed.
2. Ask *Who is speaking*? (a policeman and a woman) *What is the problem*? (Her purse/bag/money/credit cards were stolen.)
3. Put the following words on the board. Have students copy them and fill in as much information as they can.

   man:

   height
   (5′ 10″)
   weight
   (140 lbs.)
   age
   (16 or 17)
   hair
   (blonde, long, straight)
   clothing
   (jeans, T-shirt, denim vest)

   purse:

   material
   (leather)
   color
   (dark brown)
   style
   (shoulder strap)

4. Follow steps 4–12 outlined in Unit 1.

GIVE IT A TRY

1. Describing people (1)

▶ What did he look like?
▷ Well, he was fairly tall.

Pronunciation: blending of *What did he*

In rapid speech, *he* is often pronounced /e/, without the /h/. (This does not happen when *he* is the first word in an utterance or when it is stressed.) *What did he* can be pronounced /wuh-di-de/ or even /wuh-de/.

Play or read the dialog. Draw attention to the reduced pronunciation of *he* and *What did he* which are especially important in listening. Have students say the lines using /wuh-di-de/. Practice alternative forms including *What does he*/wuh-duh-ze/.

Of Interest

The words *pretty, fairly, kind of, sort of,* and *rather* all have the same general meaning of *above average or more than usual(ly)*. *Rather* is considered formal in American English. The other words are informal.

Practice

In pairs or as a class activity, have students describe several students in the room using these general descriptive terms.

2. Describing people (2)

▶ How tall was he?
▷ Around five ten, I'd say.
▶ And how much did he weigh?
▷ Around 140 pounds.

Pronunciation: review of reduced form of *he*

Play or read the dialog. Ask students how *did he* is pronounced in rapid speech and how they think *was he* and *is he* should be pronounced in rapid speech /wuh-ze/, /ih-ze/. Have students practice saying the dialog, including variations.

> **Of Interest**
>
> When we describe a person we have recently seen, we can use either the present tense or the past tense.

Practice

Group work. Before the students do the conversions, ask them to guess each other's height and weight.

3. Asking about age

▶ How old was he?
▷ Pretty young. In his mid-teens.

Pronunciation: reduced form of *his*

In rapid speech *his* is often pronounced /is/. As with *he* /e/, this does not happen when it is the first word in an utterance or when it is stressed.

Play or read the dialog. Draw attention to the pronunciation of *In his* /ih-niz/ or even /niz/. Have students practice saying the lines including the variations in their book.

Vocabulary

middle-aged: refers to a person in his/her late 40's or 50's

Practice

Pair work or group work or class work.

Extension

Ask students to guess the ages of famous people in their country, for example, the prime minister or a popular singer. The students may write their original guess on a piece of paper and compare their guesses with the other students. Have one student describe a famous person (using only physical attributes). Other students guess identity.

4. Describing hair and eyes

▶ What color is his hair?
▷ It's blond.
▶ What kind of hair does he have?
▷ It's long and straight.
▶ What color are his eyes?
▷ They are blue.

Pronunciation: review of reduced forms

Play or read the dialog. Ask students to point out places where they hear reduced forms. You might explain that reducing certain unstressed words will help them with the rhythm of English. Have students practice the dialog, working on speed and fluency.

Practice 1

Have the students look at the pictures and write their descriptions on a piece of paper. Then they can compare their descriptions with other members of the class.

Practice 2

Pair work.

5. Describing clothing

▶ What was he wearing?
▷ Jeans and a T-shirt.

Pronunciation: reduced form of *and*

In rapid speech, *and* sounds like /'n/. Play or read the dialog. Draw attention to the pronunciation of *and*. Then have students practice saying the lines, working on speed.

Practice 1

Tell the students to look at the pictures in the book for about one minute and then have them ask you or other students for the names of any items of clothing they don't know. You may want to write some or all of these words on the blackboard:
a) raincoat, (rain) hat, boots
b) dress, pocketbook/purse, (knee) socks, shoes
c) lab coat, stethoscope
d) (three-piece) suit, tie, hat, briefcase
e) (Western) shirt, vest, bandana, jeans, (cowboy) boots, (cowboy) hat
f) evening gown/long dress, necklace, earrings

Then have them close their books and write the descriptions on a piece of paper. Allow enough time for them to write as much as they remember. Then have students work in small groups, taking turns describing what the people in the illustration are wearing. The other students should listen and compare their answers.

Practice 2

Have the students look around the room for a minute

and choose one student to describe. Have them describe the student to the class trying not to look at the person.

6. Describing things
▶ What does your purse look like?
▷ It's dark brown leather, and it has a shoulder strap.

Pronunciation: stress in noun phrases

Play or read the dialog. Draw attention to the words that are stressed. Note in the second line that the adjectives preceding the noun *leather* are stressed as heavily as the noun. In contrast, where a noun precedes another noun, the first noun is more heavily stressed.

dark	brown	leather	shoulder	strap
(ADJ)	(ADJ)	(NOUN)	(NOUN)	(NOUN)

Have students practice the dialog and its variations.

Extension
Select personal items of the students in the class and ask someone to describe each one.

Practice 1
Pair work. After the students have worked in pairs, have them compare their answers with other students.

Practice 2
Model the role play with a student. Point out to the students the correct form used in the questions. Then have the students do the role-play with partners.

Extension
Have students practice the role-play based on some items they have with them (a purse, wallet, etc.). Have several pairs of students perform the role-play for the class and then show the item which was described. The other students can comment on the accuracy of the description.

LISTEN TO THIS

1.

a. Have the students look at the people in the pictures and have them describe them in their own words.

b. Play or read the conversation the first time giving students enough time to choose the correct person.
c. Play or read the conversation a second time.
d. Check students' answers.

2.

a. Have the students look at the questions in the book. Go over any unknown vocabulary words.
b. Play or read the conversation the first time and give students enough time to fill in as much information as they have understood. Do not ask for the information.
c. Play or read the conversation a second time so that students may complete the information.
d. Check students' answers.

```
LOST AND FOUND REPORT    DATE_____
ITEM  Scarf                    VALUE  $30
DESCRIPTION  Square silk scarf, red with black
             design. Two feet square
_____
LAST TIME NOTED   1:30
LAST PLACE NOTED  Coffee shop on the 5th floor
TRAVELED SINCE THEN  Shoe department
_____
IF FOUND NOTIFY: NAME  Mrs. Edna Thomas
                 ADDRESS Apartment 5B, 20 King Street
                 CITY AND STATE_____
                 PHONE  893-2124
```

UNIT 14

Have you ever been to Japan?

Setting the Scene

Ask students to describe a city they have visited. Ask questions such as: *How large was it? What were the streets like? . . . wide/narrow/clean/crowded? What kind of buildings did it have? Was the city attractive or not? In what ways? Was it interesting? What made it so?*

Vocabulary

Introduce these words now or after the students hear the conversation once.

temple: a place of religious worship

palace: a large, beautiful home usually for royalty

imperial: royal

Listening

1. Play the tape or read the conversation at normal speed.
2. Divide the class into three groups. One group will write down the words they hear describing Tokyo. The second will write down the words describing Kyoto. The third group will write down the words used in comparing Tokyo and Kyoto.
3. Let the students hear the conversation again, leaving pauses.
4. Have the students in each group combine their answers into one list. Have them write their answers on the board.

Tokyo	*Kyoto*
exciting	fascinating
not (very) attractive	beautiful temples
gray and ugly buildings	lovely gardens
crowded	old imperial temple

   Comparison

   Kyoto: smaller
   not as crowded
   more interesting
   Tokyo: more shops
   bigger selection (of things to buy)
   more expensive

5. Let the students hear the conversations again and check their answers.

GIVE IT A TRY

1. Past experiences

▶ Have you ever been to Japan?

Option 1

▷ Yes. I've been there a few times.

Option 2

▷ No, never.

Pronunciation: review of stress, intonation and rhythm

Play or read the dialog. Model and have students practice saying each line rhythmically, building up fluency.

Practice

Pair work. In order to contrast the use of the present perfect and past tenses, have students add the question *When did you . . . .* The sequence of questions and answers would then be *Have you ever . . .? Yes, I have. When did you . . .? I . . . (last year, last week, etc.)*

2. Asking for a description or opinion (1)

▶ So, what's it like?

▷ It's terrific.

Pronunciation: review of stress and rhythm

Play or read the dialog. Have students identify the words that are stressed and then practice saying these and the alternative lines as quickly and rhythmically as possible.

Of Interest

What was it like? means *What was your experience of the city?* or *How was the city when you were there?*. In contrast, *What is it like?* asks for a description of the city that would be true at all times.

Practice

Group work. Be sure that all students ask at least one question which they are then responsible for. Encourage students to expand on their answers by asking questions like *Why was it exciting?* Encourage the exchange of information and impressions in this way.

3. Asking for a description or opinion (2)

▶ What did you think of Tokyo?

▷ Exciting, but not very attractive.

▶ What are the subways like?

▷ They're clean and fast, but very crowded.

Pronunciation: intonation with *but*

In each sentence part joined by *but* there is at least one strong stress, each accompanied by rising and falling intonation.
 Play or read the dialog. Draw attention to the intonation used, especially by the second speaker. Have students practice saying the dialog, including the variations given.

Practice 1, 2, and 3

Pair work. Each student should ask and answer the questions.

Extension

After students have had enough time to ask and answer the questions as well as discuss the cities, find several people who have visited the same city and compare their impressions. Ask them to expand on their responses with examples or explanations or descriptions.

4. Comparing (1)

▶ How is Kyoto?

▷ It's smaller than Tokyo, and it's not so crowded.

▶ What are the buildings like?

▷ They're older and more beautiful than in Tokyo.

Pronunciation: review of sentence stress

Speakers emphasize the words that are most important by stressing them. In comparisons, such as those above, the qualities being compared receive stress.
 Play or read the dialog. Ask students to identify the words that are stressed. Then have them practice saying the lines, working on rhythm and fluency.

Of Interest

Students may need to be reminded of the rules concerning the formation of comparative adjectives. All one-syllable adjectives (*old, small,* etc.) and two-syllable adjectives ending in *y* (*pretty, heavy,* etc.) use *-er than* in forming the comparative. Two syllable adjectives not ending in *y* (*crowded, polite,* etc.) and all adjectives with three or more syllables (*interesting, beautiful,* etc.) use *more ... than* to form the comparative.

Practice

Pair work or group work. If groups are used be sure that all students get to ask and answer questions. If tape recorders are available, tape some off the conversations in the groups or pairs and play them back for the class. Encourage other students to make additional comparisons or disagree with the comparisons made.

5. Things to see

▶ What can you see there?

▷ There are lots of temples and some lovely gardens. It's also got an old imperial palace.

Pronunciation: stress and intonation to highlight important ideas

Each idea that a speaker wants to emphasize is stressed. Thus it is possible not only to stress *temples* and *gardens*, but also, the words *lots* and *lovely* that describe them if the speaker wishes to emphasize these ideas.

Play or read the dialog. Draw attention to the stress and intonation used by the second speaker. Then have students practice saying the lines including the alternatives in their books. Note: The second speaker's line also provides an opportunity to practice the sounds /r/ and /l/.

Practice

Pair work. Have students find out about other aspects of the towns or cities. For example, *Where do people go on Saturday night? Are there interesting or fun places to go?*

Extension

If there are two or more students from the same town, have the class ask them questions about the town. Encourage them to describe different places of interest.

6. Comparing (2)

▶ Which city is better for shopping?

Option 1

▷ Tokyo is better. It's got more shops.

Option 2

▷ Kyoto isn't as good. It doesn't have as many shops.

Pronunciation: review of sentence stress

Play or read the dialog. Have students identify the words that receive sentence stress. Then have them practice saying the dialog including the alternative line, using the rhythmic pattern set up by the stresses.

Practice

Pair work. If students don't know other cities for the comparisons, have them make general comparisons between living in large and small cities. They might compare such aspects as noise, excitement, prices of food or clothing, crime, etc. If tape recorders are available, tape one or two of the conversations and play them for the class. Then ask each student to summarize one of the comparisons s/he heard.

7. Comparing (3)

▶ Which is the most expensive?

▷ Tokyo is the most expensive city (in the world).

Pronunciation: review of stress, intonation and rhythm

Use the above lines to review stress, rhythm and intonation and work on fluency.

Of Interest

For comparisons among three or more things, all one-syllable words and those two-syllable words ending in *y* take *the -est*. Two-syllable words not ending in *y* and all words of three or more syllables take *the most* . . . .

Practice 1 and 2

Pair work or group work. Students should add other questions. For example, *What is the largest ocean in the world? The largest lake? The smallest country?* If the students don't know an answer, ask them to find out for the next class.

Extension

Have students ask and answer questions about their own country and items of interest connected with it. For example, *Which city has the largest population? Which city is the most industrial? What is the oldest city in the country?* etc. Again, if the students don't know the answers, have them find the information for the next class.

LISTEN TO THIS

1.

a. Play the tape or read the conversation the first time. Ask the students what points of information they understood just by listening.
b. Have students make two columns on a piece of paper:
   Los Angeles   San Francisco
   Tell them to write down only words or phrases which they hear to describe the cities.
c. Play or read the conversation the second time. Put the two columns on the board and ask students to give you words or phrases which they heard.

Possible answers:

Los Angeles

clean
spacious
trees
transportation problem
bus service – bad
no subway
Hollywood homes
Universal Studios
Disneyland
warm weather

San Francisco

cool weather
beautiful
hills, bay, houses
more to see and do

smaller
easier to get around
buses and streetcars
Golden Gate Park
Fisherman's Wharf
cable car

Possible answers:

Past

beaches – less crowded
quiet, peaceful
no radios, no traffic
cleaner
no cans, bottles
town – smaller
some shops, few banks, a movie theater
no fancy hotels and stores
no apartment buildings
small wooden houses

Present

soldiers, tourists
hotels
more jobs, roads, cars, pollution
higher prices
higher housing costs

Vocabulary

Hollywood: an area of Los Angeles where many famous performers live

Universal Studios: A famous film studio. Tourists can see many of the sets for the movies.

Victorian houses: houses built in the late 1800's, usually large, and with interesting architectural details

streetcars and cable cars: Both used for public transportation within cities before modern buses were developed. Streetcars were powered by electricity. Cable cars were pulled by large cables. San Francisco is famous for its cable cars, which are still in use.

2.

a. Play the tape or read the conversation the first time. Ask the students what points of information they understood just by listening.
b. Have students make two columns on a piece of paper:
Past   Present
Tell them to write down only words or phrases which they hear used to describe Honolulu.
c. Play or read the conversation the second time. Put the two columns on the board and ask students to give you words or phrases which they heard.

Variations — UNIT 15 — Variations

1. Eating out

a. The waiter/waitress can copy the order form on a piece of paper while the other students look at the menu. When the customers are ready to order, they should ask the waiter/waitress to explain items they don't understand on the menu.

b. The waiter/waitress should write down and repeat the orders as they are given.

Extension

Get copies of a real menu in English and have the students develop a similar role-play.

2. Old times

a. You may wish to do an example role-play with one student about one of the people in the activity.
   Tell students to use conversation openers such as *Well, if it isn't...! I haven't seen you for ages. How have you been?* before they begin to talk about former classmates.

b. Have the students look at the information about the people, and go over any unknown vocabulary with them before they begin the activity.

Vocabulary

cheerleaders: At football games and other sports events cheerleaders are people who encourage the crowd to show their support for their team.

prom queen: A *prom* is a formal dance held by a class in high school or college. At some proms the most beautiful girl is chosen to be *prom queen*.

UCLA: University of California, Los Angeles

Yale: Yale University

bookworm: a person who studies all the time

drop out (of school): to stop going to school before the normal time

Extension

Have the students develop a role-play of the same type but which takes place ten years from now using students from the class. Have the students make up information about classmates based on what they know about them. Then choose one or two of these role-plays and have the students act them out for the class. The information may be serious or amusing.

3. The check-up

a. Remind the students that in this role-play they will be filling out a form and therefore their oral language will be different from normal conversational English. Encourage them to use such forms as *Could you tell me your _____ please? And may I ask your _____? Could you give me your _____?*

b. Have the receptionist write down the information as it is given and then check with the patient to see that it is correct.

Extension

Do a similar role play using any medical form which may be available in English from nearby hospitals, insurance companies, or government agencies.

4. Helping a friend

a. While Student A is *choosing a friend* from the drawings in the book, have Student B look at the information he/she needs to get and decide how to ask for the information and what order to ask the questions in.

b. After Student A describes his/her friend, Student B should be able to point to the corresponding picture in the book.

Extension

Give students about two or three minutes to look around the room to notice what their classmates look like and what they are wearing. Then have each person stand back to back with the person who is sitting to their right. While not looking at each other, each student must describe the other — giving approximate height, eye color, hair color, and as many details about his or her clothing as possible. After each person has thus described his/her partner, the pair can face each other and see how accurate their descriptions were.

5. Winter vacation

a. Ask the students where they would like to go or recommend going for a winter vacation. Ask them to explain their choices.

b. Divide the class into groups of three. Each student should cover the information given about the others. When they discuss their various choices, encourage them to point out advantages, disadvantages, likes and dislikes by using such expressions as *The good thing about... is that... The problem with... is that... I really don't want to*

... *I'd really love to* ... Give each group time to decide on their final choice. Then have them explain their choice to the rest of the class.

Extension

1. Substitute popular vacation places in your country and have the groups decide where they want to go and give reasons. They should again express their likes, dislikes, and the advantages of each place. You may wish to have one or two groups do the role-play for the class and invite other comments from the listening students.
2. Ask different students for their ideal vacation spots. Where would they go? How long would they stay? What would they do there? etc.

LISTEN TO THIS

a. Have the students look at the cities. Ask what they know or think about each city based on traveling, friends, or general knowledge.
b. Play the tape or read Conversation 1. Have the students fill in the names of the correct city. Do not ask for the answers.
c. Play the tape or read Conversation 1 for the second time. Give the students time to check or complete their work.
d. Follow the same procedure for Conversations 2 and 3.
e. Check the answers by having the students compare their lists with each other.

Extension

Ask the students to compare several cities they have visited. Have them use the same points of comparison as used in the book and add other points of interest.

BOOK TWO

UNIT 1

Haven't we met before?

Setting the Scene

Say to the students: *You are at a party. You see someone you think you've met before. You are not sure of the person's name, but you think you once took a class together. How would you begin a conversation?* Get several suggestions.

Vocabulary

Students may be unfamiliar with the following vocabulary. Introduce it now or after they hear the conversations. (See Introduction)

sales conference: a meeting of sales staff to discuss ways of improving business

Listening

Conversations 1 and 2
1. Tell the students that they will hear two short conversations. Ask them to listen for the information you write on the board and to write it down on a piece of paper. Write the following on the board.
   a. the names of the two people (1. *Jim McDonald, Tom Bradshaw* 2. *Alan Baxter, Penny Jacobs*)
   b. where they met before (1. *at a sales conference* 2. *at a party/at Bert Conway's party*)
   c. when they met (1. *last year* 2. *last May*)
2. Play or read the conversations the first time. Leave some time between conversations for students to make notes.
3. Play or read the conversations again allowing time for students to write.
4. Have students check their answers with each other.
5. Have students write the answers on the board. See page 2 for additional suggestions.

Conversation 3
1. Tell the students that they will now hear someone introduce two people to each other. They need to listen for:
   a. the names of the two people (*Ellen Robbins, Ted Newman*)
   b. their occupations (*a chemist, a businessman*)
2. Play or read the conversation the first time allowing time for students to write.
3. Play or read the conversation again at normal speed while students check their answers.
4. Have students check their answers with each other.
5. Have students write the answers on the board. Now play or read all three conversations again at normal speed.

GIVE IT A TRY

1. Reintroducing yourself (1)

▶ Aren't you Jim McDonald?
▷ Yes, that's right.
▶ I believe we met at a sales conference last year. My name's Tom Bradshaw.
▷ Oh, yes. I remember. How've you been?
▶ Just fine. And you?

Pronunciation: review of *Wh*-question intonation

Play or read the dialog. Draw attention to the rising-falling intonation of *How've you been?* (See p. 3, for suggestions.) Then model and have students practice each line of dialog.

Of Interest

1. We often use the negative question form *Aren't you . . .?* when we are quite sure the answer will be *Yes. Aren't you Jim McDonald?* is similar in function to *You're Jim McDonald, aren't you?*
2. The expression *I believe* is somewhat more formal than *I think* in the context of this conversation.

Practice 1 and 2

Pair work.

2. Reintroducing yourself (2)

▶ Aren't you from Seattle?
▷ Yes, that's right.
▶ I thought so. I think we met at a conference there last year.
▷ Oh, yes, I remember. It's good to see you again.

Pronunciation: review of statement intonation

Play or read the dialog. Draw attention to the rising-falling intonation used in the statements in the second, third and fourth lines. Then have students practice saying the dialog.

Vocabulary

Before students do Practice 1, they might need to learn the following words:

dormitory: a residence, usually for college or university students, with rooms for many students

country club: a recreational club, usually private, with a golf course, dining room, tennis courts, and other facilities

Practice 1 and 2

Pair work.

3. Identifying someone and being told you are mistaken

▶ Aren't you Jim McDonald?

▷ No, I'm not.

▶ Oh, sorry.

Pronunciation: review of *yes-no* question intonation

Play or read the dialog. Draw attention to the rising intonation used in the first line. Have students practice asking this question and the alternative questions in their books and answering them properly.

Practice

Pair work or chain drill. To practice the variety of quick short responses, have various students around the room ask the questions of others, who must then answer quickly.

4. Asking whether you've met before

▶ Excuse me. Haven't we met before?

▷ I'm not sure. Have we?

▶ You work for Pan Am, don't you?

Option 1

▷ Yes, that's right.

▶ I think I met you at Bert Conway's party last May.

▷ Oh, really?

Option 2

▷ No, I don't. You must have the wrong person.

▶ Oh, sorry. Well, anyway, my name's Alan Baxter.

▷ Mine's Penny Jacobs. Nice to meet you.

Pronunciation: review of tag question intonation

Play or read the dialog. Draw attention to the intonation used in the tag question in the third line and have students practice saying that line. Let them invent a few other tag questions to ask each other. Then go back to the dialog and have students practice saying both versions of it.

> **Of Interest**
>
> Point out that *You work for Pan Am, don't you?* is equivalent to *Don't you work for Pan Am?*

Practice 1, 2, and 3

Pair work. Encourage the students to *read and look up* (See p. 3) as they practice each role-play with a few other students, switching roles.

Extension

Have half the class use their books and do a role-play with other students, who do not have books.

5. Introducing another person

▶ Have you two met before?

▷ No, I don't think we have.

▶ Well, let me introduce you, then. Ellen, this is my friend, Ted Newman.

▷ It's very nice to meet you.

● Glad to meet you.

Pronunciation: review of contrastive stress

Play or read the dialog. Draw attention to the last two lines, where the word receiving stress changes (*meet* in the first line, *you* in the second). Have students practice their lines, then the whole dialog, including variations.

Of Interest

1. When people are introduced in a social situation, we use either their first name alone or their whole names when making the introduction. When people are introduced in business situations or situations in which differences in age or status are noticeable, we generally use the person's full name (*Ellen Jones*). If the person has a special title such as *Dr.*, we use that also. *Dr. Benjamin Lock.*
2. The person doing the introduction usually gestures to the person whose name she/he is saying. The people who are introduced look at each other, smile and shake hands or nod in recognition. Men always shake hands. Women can, but do not have to. Steady eye contact and a firm handshake are signs of sincerity to English speakers.

Practice 1 and 2

Students role-play in groups of three. As you monitor, encourage students to use appropriate body language.

6. Talking about occupations

▶ Ellen's a chemist.

▷ Oh, really?

● Yes, I work for Bristol Myers. And what do you do, Ted?

▷ Oh, I'm an accountant.

Pronunciation: review of intonation

These sentences can be used to review the intonation of statements, *yes-no* questions, and *Wh-* questions. Play or read the dialog. Then have students practice saying it, including the alternative lines. Listen to their intonation and provide help where necessary.

Of Interest

In some cultures, it is considered rude to ask about a person's work when first meeting them. However, it is a common subject of first conversations with people in the United States.

Practice 1 and 2

Group work. Have the students work with the same students as before. They may make up the person's occupation or use real information about the people they are introducing.

7. Introducing another person more formally

▶ Excuse me, Ted. I'd like to introduce Ellen Peters. Ms. Peters is a chemist (at Bristol Meyers).

Pronunciation reduced form of *to*

In rapid speech, when *to* is followed by a word that begins with an unstressed vowel, it blends into the following word as in /t'introduce/. Play or read the dialog. Draw attention to the blending described here. Students can practice this blending if they wish, but its primary importance to them will be in listening comprehension. Have them practice saying the dialog including the alternative lines in their books.

Of Interest

In formal social situations or in business situations, this sequence is typical: *I'd like to introduce Ellen Peters.* (no title) *Ms. Peters is a chemist.* (title and last name only)

Practice

Have the students work in pairs or walk around the class and do the role-play with several groups of people.

LISTEN TO THIS

1.

a. Have the students look at the pictures in the book and identify the settings.
b. Play or read all four conversations without pausing and have students mark the pictures appropriately.
c. Play or read the conversations through a second time.
d. Have students check their answers using any of the procedures suggested in the Introduction.

Haven't we met before?

Answers:

[1] yes ✓ no ___ (present)

[4] yes ___ no ✓ (past or present)

[3] yes ✓ no ___ (past)   OR   [3] yes ___ no ___ (present)

[2] yes ___ no ✓ (past or present)

2.

a. Have the students look at the three pictures for Listening II and identify the settings. Then go over the words listed and explain any necessary vocabulary words in addition to the one below.
   colleagues: people who work or study together
b. Follow the same procedure as for Listening 1.
c. Ask which of the conversations in Listening 2 seems most informal. Ask the students to point out differences in the language between the formal and informal introductions they heard.

Answers:
Conversation 1:
Don McNeil – colleague

Conversation 2:
Murray Goldman – business student
Jack Anderson – economics student

Conversation 3:
Mrs. Jimenez – Marketing Department
Ms. Rosetti – International Division

UNIT 2

Would you mind telling me …?

Setting the Scene

Ask the students if they have ever had a job interview. *What kinds of questions were asked? During the interviews, did they ask any questions? What kinds?*

Vocabulary

Students may need to go over the following vocabulary items. (See Introduction.)

background: experience

position: job

firm: company

employee: worker

Listening

1. Tell the students that they will hear part of a job interview.
2. Write the following on the board and tell students to listen for the information indicated.
   a. educational background (*English major*)
   b. work experience – Name (*Loomis and Martin Law Firm*)
   Place (*Sacramento*)
   Time (*1980–1983*)
   c. salary – previous (*$1,500 a month*)
   expected (*$1,600 a month*)
   d. job benefits (*time off with pay to take college courses*)
3. Follow steps 4–12 outlined on p. 00 of this Teacher's Guide.

GIVE IT A TRY

1. Confirming information

▶ You were an English major, weren't you?

▷ Yes, that's right.

Pronunciation: special intonation

It is important that the second speaker use intonation and a tone of voice that convey interest. Women will usually do this by means of the intonation pattern shown above. Men also use this pattern, but more typically, they use regular statement intonation and convey their enthusiasm by putting extra energy into their voices. Play or read the dialog. Draw attention to the two ways of saying the second line and then have students practice the dialog.

Practice

Pair or group work. Students may work in groups and ask and answer questions which they think might be asked at a job interview. Encourage students to give additional information after the initial response. As you listen to students practice, pay special attention to the forms of the auxiliaries (do, be, have, etc.) they use.

2. Asking questions in formal situations (1)

▶ Could you tell me what kind of work experience you've had?

▷ My last position was with Loomis and Martin. That's a law firm in Sacramento. Before that, I worked for Bishop and Baldwin. That was from 1978 to 1980. And I've been doing free-lance work for the last few months.

Pronunciation: stress and intonation in connected sentences

When a speaker has several connected sentences to say, the use of stress and intonation is very important in helping the listener to understand how the sentences relate to each other.

Play or read the dialog. Then draw attention to the second speaker's use of stress and intonation. Have students practice saying the connected sentences until they are comfortable with the stress and intonation required.

Practice 1

Pair work. Give the students a few minutes to look over the information which will be asked for. Have them imagine that they have been working at a job which they would like to leave and are now looking for another job. As you walk around listening to the pairs, give any assistance necessary in forming the indirect questions.

Practice 2

Pair work. Students may use the same information they used in Practice 1, or they may make up new information about their jobs. With this exercise, encourage the interviewer to ask more questions and the interviewee to give some additional information about some of the answers.

3. Asking for clarification

▶ (And) when was that (exactly)?

▷ From nineteen-eighty to nineteen eighty-three.

Pronunciation: review of *Wh*-question and statement intonation

Play or read the dialog. Have students practice saying each line, including the variations in their books, using appropriate intonation.

Practice 1

Pair work. The interviewer should look only at the questions, and the person being interviewed should look only at the information given. You might give the interviewee a few minutes to make up another job description or to use the one developed for previous Practice exercises. Have the interviewer write down the information which she/he receives.

Practice 2 and 3

Model the exercises with one student. Encourage the students to give real answers to the questions if possible. For additional listening exercises, have one or two pairs of students do the role-play for the class, and have the class write down the information they hear and check it with the pair.

4. Asking for further information

▶ I'd like to know if the company provides opportunities for further education.

▷ Yes, you can take up to six hours a week for college courses.

Pronunciation: stress and rhythm

This long utterance provides a review of stress and rhythm. It also offers a good opportunity to develop fluency. Work on phrase groups, noticing how those syllables receiving heavy stress take more time and others with lighter stress are said very quickly.

> **Of Interest**
>
> a) The indirect question forms *I'd like to know* and *Could you tell me* are usually interchangeable.
> b) *If* and *whether* are interchangeable in indirect questions.
> c) *I'd like to know* = *I would like to know*. Students may need some additional practice with the contraction and should know that it is often difficult to hear the *'d* in normal conversation.

Practice 1 and 2

Pair work. Have the students use the *I'd like to know* and *Could you tell me* forms. Encourage the students to think of other questions they might normally ask during an interview. Point out that in an interview, asking good questions is often as important as giving good answers. If there is time, ask the students for the informal versions of the questions.

Extension

If a tape recorder is available, have several pairs of students make up a role-play based on the information in the exercises. Then record the interviews, play them for the rest of the class, and ask the students to write down the information they hear.

5. Closing an interview

▶ Well, I've enjoyed meeting and talking with you. We'll call you within the week.

▷ Thank you. I appreciate the time you have given me. I look forward to hearing from you.

Pronunciation: stress and intonation

Play or read the dialog. Draw attention to the stress and intonation the second speaker uses. Then have students practice saying these lines using the same intonation.

Of Interest

The verb phrase *look forward to* is followed by the gerund form (*hearing*).

Practice

Students may use the same information and questions which they used in Exercise 4, or they may create a new job and ask different questions.

LISTEN TO THIS

1. Have the students look at the interview form. Go over any vocabulary words necessary.
2. Play or read the conversation the first time. Have the students write down as much information as they can. Do not ask for the information.
3. Play or read the conversation the second time giving the students time to fill out the form.
4. Have the students compare their answers in small groups. Then check the answers.
   Name (*Helen Ann Norcross*)
   College major (*English*)
   School (*San Francisco State College*)
   Year (*1980*)
   Present employer (*Singapore Airlines*)
   Duties (*ticket sales*)
   Length of service (*4 years*)
   Present salary (*$1,100 a month*)
   Expected salary (*not given*)
5. Play or read the conversation a third time and have students write down the actual questions the interviewer uses. It may be necessary for you to stop once or twice in order to give the students enough time to write the questions they hear.

Answers:
1) I wonder if you'd mind telling me your full name, please?
2) And could you tell me what kind of office experience you've had?
3) And would you mind telling me your present salary?

IF YOU HAVE TIME . . .

This exercise combines elements practiced in Units 1 and 2. A and B meet by chance on an airplane. They used to work at the same company. B left a few years ago to take a better job at another company. There is a job open there, and B thinks A would like it. A and B re-introduce themselves and B says, *We've got a position open that I think you might be interested in*. A then asks B for details. Students can prepare for this by reviewing Units 1 and 2 and using details from jobs described in various sections to make up the new job.

For additional ideas, see the ideas given in the *If you have time* section corresponding to Unit 2 of Book 1.

UNIT 3

Isn't he the one who . . . ?

Setting the Scene

Have the students look at the picture on the first page of Unit 3. Ask *What do you think is happening*? Accept various views, but pursue answers which fit the context of the conversation. For instance, if a student says *The women are talking*, you might ask *What do you think they're talking about*?

Vocabulary

You may wish to present the following vocabulary items.

guy: informal for man

penthouse apartment: an apartment on the top floor of a building, often more luxurious and expensive than other apartments

What's he like?: What kind of person is he?

Listening

1. Play or read the conversation the first time.
2. Put the following items on the board. Tell students to write brief answers for them.
   a) the man's name (*Bob Wilson*)
   b) his job (*airlines employee/British Airways*)
   c) his personality (*nice, friendly, sense of humor*)
   d) Married? (*yes*)
   e) Children? (*no*)
   f) How will they meet him? (*invite him and his wife over*)
3. Play or read the conversation a second time giving students time to write down as much information as they can.
4. Follow steps 4–12 outlined on page 2.

GIVE IT A TRY

1. Asking who someone is

▶ Do you know who that guy is?
▷ Which one?
▶ The one in the light slacks.

Option 1
▷ Oh, that's Bob Wilson. He's the one who just moved into the penthouse apartment.

Option 2
▷ I have no idea.

Pronunciation: blending in *Do you*

In rapid speech *do you* is pronounced /d'yuh/. Play or read the dialog. Draw attention to the blended form. Have students work on saying the first line as quickly as possible and then continue, practicing both versions of the conversation, including the variations in their books.

Practice

Pair work. Encourage the students to vary their responses by identifying some people by their physical characteristics, some by apartment numbers, some by their places of business, some by their cars, etc.

2. Asking about someone

▶ Do you know where he's from?
▷ I think he's from England.

Pronunciation: review of reduced form of *he*

In rapid speech *he* is frequently reduced to /e/. Play or read the dialog. Draw attention to the rhythm of the first line with its stressed and unstressed words and to the reduced form of *he*. Have students practice saying this line rhythmically and then continue with the rest of the dialog, including the variations in the student's book.

Practice 1

Use one of the pictures to model the role-plays with a student. Then have pairs of students work with the other pictures. Have the students take both parts during the pair work. Encourage them to ask other questions about the people in the pictures.

Practice 2

Model the dialog with one of the students. Use any student in the class as an example. Then have pairs of students talk about other members of the class.

3. Asking about someone's personality

▶ What's he like?
▷ He seems like a (very) nice guy.

Pronunciation: blending of *What's he*

In rapid speech *What's he* sounds like /wut-ze/. Play or read the dialog. Draw attention to the reduced form. Have students practice it and then continue with the rest of the dialog, doing each version and using all of the vocabulary. Ask the students for other adverbs they might use in place of *very*, *pretty*, and *rather* in line 1. (Some possibilities are *fairly* and *really*.) Have the students practice using these words in the sentences.

Vocabulary

You may need to go over some of the following vocabulary items.

outgoing: very friendly and talkative
moody: having moods that often change; unfriendly

Practice

Draw attention to the "vocabulary box" on the right and explain any words your students do not know. Use one of the pictures to model the dialog with a student. If the students have difficulty in describing the people in the pictures, have them choose some well-known people to describe.

outspoken: quick to give his/her own opinion
arrogant: acting as if she/he were superior to others

Ask students what qualities they like/dislike in people and help them with any new vocabulary they may need to express these ideas.

4. Identifying someone

▶ Is he the one whose wife has the green Volvo?

Option 1
▷ Yeah, that's right.

Option 2
▷ No, I don't think so.

Pronunciation: blending of *Is he*

In rapid speech *Is he* is pronounced /ih-ze/ or it is reduced to /ze/. Knowing this will help students in listening, and can also help them to work on speed and fluency in their own speech. Play or read the dialog. Draw attention to the blending in the first line and practice that line, working for speed and fluency. Continue with the dialog, practicing both versions.

Of Interest

In this exercise the students can see the difference between the positive and negative forms of the questions. Ask the students which form they would use if they were almost sure that the answer were *Yes*. (answer: *Isn't she* . . .)

Practice 1

Pair work. Before the students do the exericse, you can help them prepare as follows: Pointing to the first picture in the Student Book say, "Her husband plays the drums." Then write on the board:

   She's the one _____.

Wait for the students to offer the correct words and then write them in: (*whose husband plays the drums*). Now ask them to look for the same woman in the party scene below. On the board write:

   Isn't she the one _____?

Wait for students to offer the completion and write it in. Now have them read the instructions for the exercise again and practice in pairs.

Practice 2

Pair work. Before the students do the dialog, write one fact about a member of your family on the board and model the dialog with one student. For example, *My mother goes shopping every day*.

Extension

Have two or three pairs do their dialogs in front of the class, and ask the class where the student had met the relative before.

5. Asking about personal details

▶ Do you know if they have any children?

Pronunciation: rhythm

This model provides a good example of the typical rhythm of English which results from the regular alternation of stressed and unstressed syllables. Tap out the beat as you model and have students practice this sentence. Then, ask students to suggest other sentences that would fit the same rhythm. (They may simply change the words *children* or *have*.) Finally, practice the alternate sentence in the Student Book.

Isn't he the one who...?

Practice

Pair work or group work. Have the pairs or groups ask about students not in their pair or group. Encourage the students to ask other questions in addition to those suggested in the book.

LISTEN TO THIS

1.

a. Have the students look at the picture and try to guess where each person is from. Ask the students what questions they would ask in order to identify the person they are asking about. For example, *Who is the man with the moustache? Who is the woman in the long dress?*

b. Play or read the conversation the first time and have the students draw circles around the countries they hear. (Or, have them write the names of the countries on a piece of paper.)

c. If the class has difficulty catching the names of many of the countries, pronounce the names of the countries listed in their books and then play the tape again before asking for the countries.

d. Have students check answers with each other, and then ask for the names of the countries. (*Australia, India, Taiwan, Indonesia, Nigeria, Mexico.*)

e. Play or read the conversation again and have the students draw a line from the person to his/her name.

f. Play or read the conversation again and have the students write the name of the country they are from.

g. Have the students compare their answers in small groups. Then, check their answers.

2.

a. Have the students look at the pictures of the men and identify each of their professions.
b. Play or read the conversation and have the students draw a line from the woman's name to the man in the picture.
c. Play or read the conversation a second time and give students time to finish the assignment.
d. Have the students compare their answers in small groups.

Vocabulary

beats me: I have no idea.

IF YOU HAVE TIME ...

First, divide the students into pairs. Their first task is to make up some information about a man and a woman (to "create" two people). Then, have students change partners and use the information in the following situation. Tell the students: *You are at a party with a friend. You see someone you don't know come in. You ask your partner about the person.*

UNIT 4

Where exactly is it?

Setting the Scene and Vocabulary

This Unit contains many vocabulary items used in giving directions. In order to introduce or review them, you might want to draw a map of the area around your class building. Include a few buildings on your map. Here is a list of the terms used in giving directions which appear in the Conversation and Practices.

parallel to	near
crosses	just past
at the end of	just before
down the (street or corridor)	to your right/left
next to	the rear – the back

Write these words on the board next to the map and have students make up sentences about the map using the vocabulary.

Listening

1. Have students look at the map in their books while you play or read the conversation the first time.
2. Write the following on the board for students to copy on a piece of paper.
   a. Washington Street ____(crosses)____ Main.
   b. It's ____(parallel to)____ Thompson.
   c. The Shell Building is ____(just past)____ the post office.
   d. The camera shop is on the ____(ground)____ floor ____(next to)____ the entrance.
3. Play or read the conversation the second time. Give the students time to fill in the direction words for a – d.
4. Check the answers.

Play or read the dialog. Draw attention to the rapid pronunciation of *Is there*, which is especially important for listening comprehension. Have students practice saying each line of the dialog including the alternate words. Students should work on rhythm and fluency.

Practice 1

Before the students do the dialog, have them look at the names of the stores and say what kind of service they would find in each. Then have them do the dialog in pairs or in groups of three. Remind students to use the indirect question form.

Practice 2

Have the students look at the map of the hotel lobby in their books and ask them what they would expect to find in each of the shops listed. Tell them that they are standing at the information booth when they are asking the questions. Students then do the exercise in pairs.

Practice 3

Ask the students about various kinds of shops in the area of the school and what they can get in those shops. Ask if they know the names of the streets which the shops are on. Students can then do the exercise in pairs or in groups. Have them think of other services they might want to know about and add them to the list in the book. If there is no place nearby which offers the services, their response would be *I don't think there's any place nearby where you can . . . .*

GIVE IT A TRY

1. Asking where facilities and services are located

▶ Is there a place near here where I can get my camera repaired?

▷ I think there's a camera shop on Washington Street.

Pronunciation: blending of *Is there*

In rapid speech, *Is there* is pronounced /zthere/ or even /zere/. (This is in contrast to the pronunciation of *there's*, which, even in rapid speech, keeps the initial /th/ sound.)

2. Locating streets

▶ Is that the street that runs parallel to Foster?

▷ No, it crosses Foster.

Pronunciation: contrastive stress

This model can be used to demonstrate contrastive stress. In the second line, the stress falls on *crosses* rather than on *Foster* (which is the last stressed word in the utterance) because the speaker wants to emphasize the most important piece of information he

is giving: *The street crosses Foster. (It doesn't run parallel.)*
Play or read the dialog. Ask students where they hear the stress in each line. Then have them practice saying the dialog.

Practice 1

Review *runs into*, *is off*, *turns into*, *is parallel to*, and *crosses* by having the students look at the map while you read the sentences which apply: *Which street runs into Broadway? Is Fox Street off Broadway? Does Broadway turn into Grange?* etc. Use some questions which will involve negative responses, such as *Is Fox Street parallel to Broadway?* Then have the students work in pairs or small groups to do the exercise.

Practice 2

Pair work or small groups.

3. Asking for specific locations

▶ Where on Washington Street is it?

▷ It's in the Shell Building.

Pronunciation: sentence stress

Note that the sentence stress in the first line falls on *is*, rather than on any of the content words.
   Play or read the dialog. Draw attention to the intonation. Then have students practice saying each line, using appropriate stress and intonation. (Note: In the alternate for line 2 — *214 Washington Street* — the stress falls on the first syllable of *Washington*.)

Practice

Model the dialog with a student. Then have the students work in pairs. Remind them to switch roles.

Extension

After the students have practiced the dialog, have them close their books and listen to two students do the dialog. The other students should write down the phone numbers and addresses they hear. Then have them check them with the "operator" who gave the information.

4. Identifying buildings by appearance and location

▶ Which one is the Shell Building?

▷ It's the big glass office building just past the post office.

Pronunciation: stress in NOUN NOUN combinations

This model can be used to review the stress pattern for NOUN NOUN combinations: the first, modifying noun receives stronger stress than the second, as in *Shell Building*, *office building*, *post office*, and *subway entrance*.
   Play or read the dialog. Draw attention to the above stress pattern. Then have students practice these lines and the ones in their books, being careful to stress the appropriate words.

Practice

Have the students look at the map and first describe the buildings. Then have them give directions based on nearby sites or buildings. For example, *The Shell Building is a big glass office building. It's next to the post office.* Then have the students work in pairs or in groups to do the exercise.

5. Asking where inside a building something is located

▶ And what floor is the camera shop on?

Option 1

▷ On the ground floor next to the entrance.

Option 2

▷ It's upstairs, on the third floor.

Pronunciation: review

This model can be used to review stress, intonation, and rhythm. Play or read the dialog. Have students listen for the syllables on which the voice rises and falls. Have them listen again for the words which receive stress. Then have them say the lines, using appropriate stress and intonation.

Where exactly is it?

Practice 1

Pair work. Students may need to review the following vocabulary items before they do the dialog.

household appliances: refrigerators, stoves, washing machines, etc.

accounts section: in a department store the section which deals with credit card customers

Practice 2

Students may need to review the following vocabulary items before they do the dialog.

Registrar's Office: the office where students sign up (register) for classes or change classes.

Student Services: the office that gives students information about student activities, housing, jobs, transportation, etc.

Model the dialog with one student. Then ask what other services students usually need at a school and where those services are found. Then have the students do the dialog in pairs.

6. Asking about opening/closing times (1)

▶ Do you know how long it's open?

▷ It stays open till five thirty.

Pronunciation: stress when telling time

Note in the second line that the stress falls on *thirty* rather than on *five*. When giving the time, speakers put the greatest stress on the last number (eg. *five fifteen, five oh five*). Play or read the dialog. Ask students to listen for the stress in the second line. Then have them say each line including the alternate lines in their books.

Practice 1

Pair work or chain drill. If you wish to do the exercise as a chain drill, have half the class look at and read only student A's part and the other half look at and read only Student B's part.

Practice 2

Pair work. To have the students prepare for and expand on this exercise, list six or seven well-known places in your town or city on the board. For each of the places, have one student ask the question and another student give the answer. If the student doesn't know the answer, have him/her say *Sorry, I don't know*. When the list and hours are completed, have the students practice in pairs.

7. Asking about opening/closing times (2)

▶ Is the club open in the evening?

Option 1
▷ Yes, I think so.

Option 2
▷ I don't think so.

Pronunciation: two ways to say *the*

The is pronounced /thuh/ before consonants: (*the club*) and /thee/ before vowels: (*the evening*).

Draw attention to these two pronunciations, giving additional examples if necessary. Then play or read the dialog and have students practice saying it, including all of the variations in their book. In order to have the students practice the prepositional phrases of time, introduce additional expressions as necessary. Substitute different days and times until students can use the prepositions confidently.

Of Interest

The expressions *in the evening* and *evenings* are interchangeable, as are *on the weekend* and *weekends*. However, *on Saturday* may mean *this Saturday* or *every Saturday*, while *Saturdays* means only *every Saturday*.

Practice 1 and 2

Pair work. Have students switch parts as they practice each dialog.

Practice 3

Pair work. Have the students use buildings from their own town or city. Then have one or two pairs act out their dialog for the class. Ask the other students questions about the days and times they heard.

LISTEN TO THIS

1.
a. Have students read the directions and look at the map in their books.
b. Play the conversation for the first time. Students just listen.
c. Play or read the conversation a second time. This time students label each of the locations on their maps by drawing a line to it.
d. Have students compare their work.

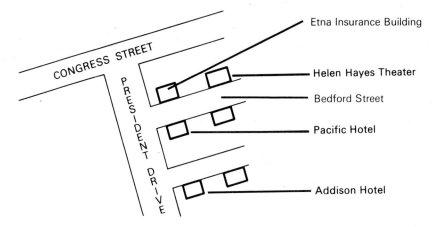

2.
a. Have students read the directions and look at the map in their books.
b. Have them describe one or two of the buildings.
c. Play or read the conversation the first time. Students listen.
d. Play or read the conversation the second time. Give the students enough time to identify the buildings.
e. Have the students compare their maps in small groups.

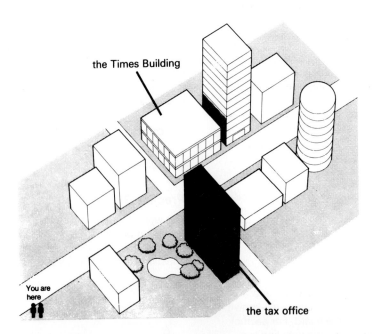

3.

a. Have the students look at the questions for this section. Go over any necessary vocabulary words.
b. Play or read the conversation for the first time. Have the students put *T* or *F* next to the statements concerning Conversation 1.
c. Play or read the first conversation for the second time. Give students time to complete or to check their work.
d. Follow the same procedure for the remaining conversations.
e. Check the answers to the comprehension questions.

Answers:
1. a. T
   b. F (from 9 a.m. to 9 p.m.)
2. a. F (It is closed on Thursdays.)
   b. T
3. a. F (It is closed on weekends.)
   b. F (The office closes at 5:30.)
4. a. F (The club is open 24 hours a day.)
   b. T
5. a. T
   b. F (It is open only on weekdays.)

4.

a. Have the students read the directions and look at the list of departments. Go over the pronunciation of each and explain any vocabulary which students may not know.
   Customer Service: the department which deals with refunds, exchanges, and complaints.
b. Play or read the first conversation a first time. Give students time to draw the line from the department to the floor.
c. Play or read the first conversation a second time and give students time to check their decision.
d. Follow the same procedure for the remaining conversations.
e. Check the answers to the questions by asking the students which floor each department is on.

Answers:
Accounts Department – 5th floor
Children's Department – 1st floor
Customer Service – 3rd floor
Sporting Department – 4th floor
Garden Shop – 2nd floor

IF YOU HAVE TIME ...

Have each student prepare a small map of an area they lived in some time ago. Tell them to include a few streets and building locations. They should not show their maps to others. Divide the class into groups of two or three. As one student describes his/her map, the other(s) should try to draw a sketch of it. Encourage those drawing to ask questions to confirm they are correct as they go along.

When the first map is complete, have students in the pair or threesome compare what they have drawn with the original. Then, let another student describe his/her map until everyone has had an opportunity to both describe and draw.

Variations — UNIT 5 — Variations

1. Society Column

a. Divide the class into groups which include students who have not worked together in previous units. Before the students do the exercise, role-play a typical introduction and opening conversation. Draw attention to the body language involved.

b. During the activity, encourage the students to use any "real" information they know about each other. For example, *Don't you usually eat lunch in the cafeteria around noon? I think I've seen you there with some other students from class.* Students should get out of their seats and move around for this, acting out their roles with all of the body language that would be natural in this situation.

c. After the students have done the activity, ask them to name and give one interesting fact about different class members.

2. Do you know ..."

a. Before the class does the activity, review indirect question forms. For example, *Do you know if he/she is married? Do you know where he/she lives?*

b. Divide the class into groups of three or more for this activity. In addition to asking about you, students can continue to ask questions and exchange information about other students or about well-known people (entertainers, politicians, etc).

c. Bring the whole class together and let students ask any questions they couldn't get the answer to earlier. Have each group tell about any of the additional people they talked about. Encourage other students to ask questions about that person.

3. Getting to know you

a. Have the students do the activity with someone they have not worked with before. Encourage the students to elaborate on their answers and questions and to ask other questions which might be of interest. For example, *What kinds of books do you like to read? Do you like movies? What kinds?* As you monitor the pairs, encourage a natural flow of conversation by asking your own questions and encouraging the students to elaborate.

b. After the students have finished the activity, have a few of them tell the class some interesting fact about their partners.

4. Interview

a. Before the students look at the exercise in the book, ask some questions based on the information students have given in previous exercises. Use such question forms as *I understand that (you like football). Is that right?/ You want to study engineering in college, don't you?/ I heard that you have two children.* Encourage the students to give real answers such as *Well, no. I want to study computer science./ Yes, that's right. I have two daughters.*

b. Have students cover their partners' cues when they do the activity. Have the "reporter" write down the information they hear and check it with "Mr. Montovani" when they have finished the activity.

Extension

Have the students work in groups of three or four to develop an interview with a famous historical person from their country's history or from world history. Then have them perform their interview for the class.

5. Finding Your Way

A.

1. Before the students begin the activity, review the expressions of location in the student book, illustrating them on the board if necessary.

2. When the students do the activity, only Student B will look at the map. As Student B describes the location, Student A should repeat the information given or write it down and read it back to Student B, who will confirm or correct it.

Extension

If city maps are available for your town or city, give them to Student B. Write the names of some streets on the board and have Student A ask for their locations. When Student B gives the location, Student A should write down the location or repeat it. Then have Student A's from different pairs write the information they got on the blackboard so that students can compare different ways of describing locations to see which is clearest.

B.
1. Before the students do the activity, review common expressions used in giving directions. For example, *between _____ Street and _____ Street; near the corner of _____; one block down from _____*, etc. Students can refer to Unit 4 for additional vocabulary.
2. Only Student B should look at the map. As Student B describes the location, Student A should repeat the information given so that Student B can confirm it.

Extension

For additional practice, write the names of several well-known buildings in your town or city on the board and ask the students to explain where they are.

UNIT 6

You'd better get some rest.

Setting the Scene

Have the students look at the picture at the beginning of Unit 6. Ask questions about the picture. For example, *What seems to be wrong with the woman in the picture? What advice would you give her? What is the best advice to give someone who has a headache? a fever? a cold?*

Vocabulary

You may need to go over the following vocabulary items.

fever: body temperature above normal

take it easy: relax

Listening

1. Play the tape or read the conversation a first time.
2. Put the following questions on the board.
   a. What's wrong with Joan? (*She has a fever and a headache.*)
   b. How has she already tried to help herself? (*with aspirin*)
   c. Why hasn't she gone to a doctor? (*She hates them.*)
   d. What does Betty suggest? (*Take aspirin. Stay in bed. Take it easy.*)
   e. Will Joan finish reading her article first? (*No/probably not*)
3. Follow steps 4–12 outlined on page 2.

GIVE IT A TRY

1. Asking what the matter is

▶ What's the matter?

▷ I've got a fever and a really bad headache.

▶ Oh, that's a shame.

Pronunciation: special intonation

Play or read the dialog. Draw attention to the intonation of the last line. Have students practice it and then the alternate lines: *That's too bad* and *I'm sorry to hear that.* Then have them practice the entire dialog.

Practice

Pair work or chain drill. First ask the students for other possible physical problems. Write them on the board and have the students practice with them as well as those listed in their books.

2. Giving tentative advice (1)

▶ Why don't you take some aspirin?

▷ I've already tried that, but it didn't help.

Pronunciation: tone of voice

This model can be used to show how a tone of voice helps to convey attitude.

Play or read the dialog. Draw attention to the difference between the voice of the advice giver, who is trying to be cheerful, and that of the sick person, who is feeling sad. Have students practice the dialog, including variations, trying to use their voices in a similar way to convey appropriate attitudes. Note: Some advice givers would speak differently than this one, using their voice to convey sympathy rather than cheer.

> **Of Interest**
>
> The forms *Why don't you . . .* and *Maybe you should . . .* are friendlier and more helpful in tone than *you should*, which can sound rather bossy.

Practice

Pair work. First model the dialog with one student. Then have the students work in pairs.

Vocabulary

You may need to go over the following vocabulary items before the students practice the dialog:

lozenges: medicated hard candy used to relieve a sore throat

bicarbonate: a bubbling liquid used to relieve stomach pains

cold capsules: capsules containing medication which relieve cold symptoms

Extension

Ask the students for other physical problems and possible remedies for them. List them on the board and have the students include them in their pair work. Ask them if they know any traditional or folk remedies.

3. Giving tentative advice (2)

▶ Maybe you should see a doctor.
▷ Yes, I suppose I should.

Pronunciation: tone of voice

Play or read the dialog, which, like the previous one, shows people in two different emotional states. Ask students to identify any features they may notice about the voices. Then have them try to use their voices to convey the appropriate emotion as they practice the dialog and its variations.

Of Interest

I suppose I should does not mean that the person will follow the advice which is given. It simply means that he/she knows that it is well-intentioned.

Practice 1

Chain drill or class work. Have one student take Student A's part and another student take Student B's part. Repeat as many times as you think necessary

Practice 2

Pair work. Remind students to use both *Why don't you* and *Maybe you should ...*

Extension

Ask students for other situations in which advice is often given. For example, problems with the car, problems at school, problems with the family. Have students think of typical problems in these areas and typical solutions to them. Then have pairs develop a dialog based on these problems. Call on one or two pairs to perform their dialogs for the class. Ask the class if there is any other advice which might have been given.

4. Giving advice (1)

▶ You'd (really) better get some rest.
▷ Yes, that sounds like a good idea. I will.

Pronunciation: reduced form of *you'd better*

In rapid speech, *you'd better* sounds like /yuhd-bed-der/ or even /ya-bed-der/. Play or read the dialog. Draw attention to the rapid pronunciation of *you'd*

better. Have them practice the dialog including variations, using the less reduced form /yuhd-bed-der/.

Of Interest

You'd better is the contraction for *you had better.* This does not refer to the past tense, and is used interchangeably with *you ought to* and *you should.*

Practice 1 and 2

Model the dialog with a student. Then have the students work in pairs. For Practice 2, the students must give their own advice. After the students have practiced both exercises, have one or two pairs of students do the dialog for Practice 2. Then ask other students what advice was given, and ask if there is any other advice they might want to add.

5. Giving advice not to do something

▶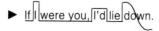

▷ Yes, I guess you're right.

Pronunciation: intonation for emphasis

The voice rises on *really* to give emphasis to the utterance. Play or read the dialog. Draw attention to the intonation. Then have students practice saying the lines, using the intonation illustrated.

Practice 1

Pair or class work.

Practice 2

Group work. Have the students work in groups of three. One student states the problem and the other two students give some advice. Encourage students to devise other problems and to offer typical advice, or to exchange advice on problems they are having now.

6. Giving advice (2)

▶ If I were you, I'd lie down.
▷ Yes, that sounds like good advice.

Pronunciation: intonation in complex sentences.

In sentences of more than one clause, each clause has a strong sentence stress accompanied by a rise in pitch. The stress in the above *if* clause falls on *I*. (In other contexts, it could fall on *you*.)

Play or read the dialog. Draw attention to the intonation of the first line and then of the alternate sentence:

What I would do is lie down.

Then have students practice saying the dialog, including the variations.

Of Interest

1. In the present unreal conditional, *were* is always used for the verb *be* (*If I/you/he/she/it/we/they **were** . . . .*) Other verbs use the usual form of the past tense.
2. *I'd lie down = I would lie down.*

Practice

Group work. First model the dialog with a student. Then divide the class into groups of three. One student will act as the advisor, and the other students will ask the questions. Then they should switch roles.

Extension

After the students finish with the role-play, have the groups work on giving advice about a place one (or more) of them has visited. They may use the questions given in the original role-play and should make up other questions which are common when asking advice about visiting some place. For example, *Where should I go at night? Are there any interesting places I should visit? Are there some places I shouldn't go?*

LISTEN TO THIS

1.

a. Have the students look at the comprehension questions before they listen to the conversation.
b. Play or read the conversation for the first time. Tell the students to give short answers to the questions on a sheet of paper. Give the students time to write down as much as they have understood.
c. Play or read the conversation for the second time. Give the students enough time to complete or correct their answers.
d. Check the answers.

Answers:
1. (She has) a headache.
2. (She has) to finish a report by 3:00.
3. Yes. (She took) aspirin.
4. (She's going to) go home.

Vocabulary
splitting headache: very bad headache. This adjective is used only with *headache*.

2.

Follow the same procedure as in Listening 1.

Answers:
1. (He) can't sleep.
2. (for) about two months.
3. No.
4. (He is) working too hard. (He works 10–11 hours a day.)
5. change jobs (Change to a less stressful job.) Slow down.

IF YOU HAVE TIME . . .

Divide the class into groups of 4. Give a different problem to a student in each group. Have the others offer advice. If you have time, students can change groups for further practice.

a) A friend gave you a shirt/blouse as a birthday present. It's too small.
b) Your boss has given you an extra assignment. It's due in a week. You already have a lot of work to complete.
c) You are at a friend's house for dinner. As you are helping in the kitchen, you accidentally drop the friend's favorite serving platter, a gift from her grandmother.
d) You are riding a taxi. The driver is driving too quickly and you are getting more and more nervous.
e) You are going to take a long plane trip. You don't want to be too tired at the end of it.
f) Your neighbors play their stereo very loudly. It disturbs you.

UNIT 7

Do I need to …?

Setting the Scene

Have the students look at the picture at the beginning of the unit. Ask *Why do you think the student is at the U.S. embassy? Do you know anyone who has ever applied to a foreign university? What did they need to do?*

Vocabulary

It may be necessary to review the following vocabulary items.

school records: official documents listing the courses you have taken and your grades

letter of recommendation: a letter supporting a person's application to a school or for a job

affidavit: a legal written statement

TOEFL: test of English proficiency given to foreign students

SAT: Scholastic Aptitude Test of language and mathematical ability

I-20: an official document given to a foreign student by a U.S. college or university saying that he/she is a full-time student at that institution

Listening

1. Play or read the conversation for the first time.
2. Write these key words on the blackboard and pronounce them. Then leave them on the board so that students can refer to them. application affidavit   proof of financial support recommendation   TOEFL   SAT   acceptance   I-20
3. Now have students listen again and take notes on the steps the embassy offical gives Yoko. As you play the tape, be sure to pause so that students have enough time to write.

    ### Answers
    a. write and get application form
    b. send it with copy of school records and affidavit/proof of financial support
    c. get letters of recommendation
    d. take TOEFL and maybe SAT
    e. get acceptance and I-20 form
    f. apply for visa
4. Play or read the conversation again while students check their answers.
5. Have the students check their answers in small groups. Have each group combine information and make one list of steps. Let them compare their list with those of other groups.

GIVE IT A TRY

1. Asking the procedure

▶ I'd like some information on how to get into an American university.

▷ Well, first you write and get an application form. Then you send it in with a copy of your school records and an affidavit of support. And after that you ask your teachers for some letters of recommendation.

Pronunciation: intonation of sequential items

There is a strong sentence stress and a rise in intonation on each word or phrase used to signal a new step in a sequence (*First, then, after that*).

Play or read the dialog. Draw attention to the intonation used. Then have students practice the dialog, making sure to follow the intonation pattern for items in a sequence.

Practice 1

Pair work and class work. Divide the class into pairs and assign one of the procedures to each pair. Give the students enough time to put the steps in order and to practice the dialog. Then choose one pair of students for each procedure and have them act out the dialog for the class. As they give the steps, the other students can number the steps in their books.

Practice 2

Pair work and class work. Have several pairs choose one procedure for which they will list the steps in the same way they did Practice 1. In addition to the procedures listed in the book, take suggestions from the class for other activities. For example: how to start a car, how to write a simple business letter, or how to start a fire. Give the students time to develop and list the steps. Then have one pair give the steps for each procedure to the rest of the class. The other students will list the steps as they hear them. Then have the students check the procedure.

2. Asking what the requirements are

▶ Do I need to take any tests?

Option 1
▷ Yes, you have to take the TOEFL examination.

Option 2
▷ No, you don't have to.

Pronunciation: *to* in terminal positon

Like other function words, *to* is usually reduced but not when it is in the terminal position. Note the contrast between *to*, said very lightly and quickly as /tuh/ in the first two lines and more slowly, as /too/, in the third.
 Play or read the dialog. Draw attention to the pronunciation of *to* in each line. Then have students practice each line, including variations.

Practice 1 and 2

Pair work and class work. Divide the class in half and divide each half into pairs. Assign half the class Practice 1 and the other half Practice 2. Give the students time to develop a dialog using the information given and the patterns which have been practiced. Then, have all the students make two columns on a piece of paper:
Required   Not Required
 Have one pair of students from Practice 1 do their dialog for the other students. The students who have done Practice 2 should write down the information they hear under the appropriate columns. Have another pair from Practice 1 do their dialog so that the other students can check or complete their lists. Then, have the students who have taken notes check the answers with other pairs who have done Practice 1. Next, have a pair of students who worked on Practice 2 read their dialog and repeat the procedure.

3. Asking whether something is permitted/recommended

▶ Is it all right to apply to several universities?

Option 1
▷ Yes, sure.

Option 2
▷ No, you shouldn't.

Pronunciation: *to* before vowels and consonants

Before vowels, *to* is pronounced /too/ when not reduced and /t'/ when reduced. Before consonants, it is pronounced /tuh/. Play or read the dialog. Draw attention to the pronunciation of *to*. Then have students practice the dialog, including variations.

Practice 1

It may be necessary to go over the following vocabulary items before the students do this exercise.
obligatory: required
surrender: hand in to the authorities
issue: give
valid: legal to use at the present time

Practice 2

Pair work. First have the students look over the regulations and discuss any points which are not clear. Then have them ask and answer the questions in pairs.

4. Asking when it is possible to do something

▶ When can I apply for a visa?

▷ You won't be able to apply for a visa until you've gotten a letter of acceptance.

Pronunciation: rhythm

The first sentence provides a good example of the rhythmic pattern that results from the alternation of stressed words with unstressed ones.
 Play or read the dialog. Ask students which words are stressed and which reduced. Tap out the stresses and have them practice the first line rhythmically. Do the same for the alternate to line one in the Student Book. Then continue practicing the dialog.

Practice

Pair or class work. If you wish to do this exercise as a class activity, skip around the room and have one student ask and one student answer the question.

5. Asking about rules/regulations

▶ Are foreign students allowed to work?

Option 1
▷ No, you're not.

Option 2
▷ Yes, you are, but only in the summer.

Do I need to ...?

Pronunciation: intonation of short answers

This model can be used to introduce the stress and intonation used in short answers. Play or read the dialog. Draw attention to the stress and intonation used in the second speaker's lines. Then have students practice the dialog.

Practice 1

Pair work and class work. Divide the class into pairs and have the students cover the part they will not be using. After getting the answer from "the librarian," the "student" can write down *Yes* or *No* next to the question in the book.

Practice 2

Pair work and class work. Have each pair ask and answer the questions in the book as well as four new questions and answers which tourists often ask. When the pairs have practiced the question and answers, the students can share their additional questions with the class.

LISTEN TO THIS

1.

Part 1

a. Have the students look at the pictures in their books. Go over any necessary vocabulary words.
b. Give the students a few minutes to predict the order they think they will hear, numbering the pictures sequentially.

Part 2

a. Play or read the conversation. Tell students to use the information they hear to correct or confirm their predictions.
b. Play or read the conversation the second time.
c. Have the students compare their answers in groups of three.

Answers:

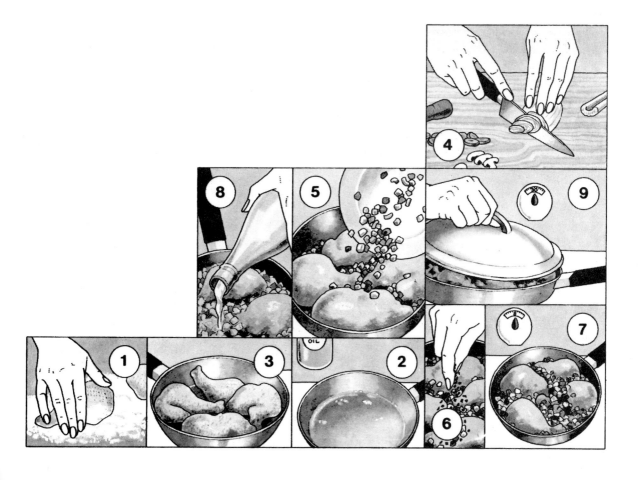

2.

a. Have the students look at the statements in their books. Explain any necessary vocabulary words.
b. Play or read the conversation the first time. Do not ask for the answers.
c. Play or read the conversation the second time and give the students time to complete or check their work.
d. Go over answers to the comprehension questions.

Answers:

	Permitted	Not Permitted
1. Residents may park . . .	×	
2. Guests may park . . .		×
3. Residents can have a dog . . .		×
4. Residents may place garbage . . .		×
5. Regular paper bags . . .	×	

Vocabulary

residents: people who live in a place. *The residents of a town; the residents of an apartment building,* etc.

IF YOU HAVE TIME . . .

Sometimes it is difficult to tell someone how to perform an everyday task. (For instance, tell step by step how to tie shoelaces or how to ride a bicycle.) Ask students for examples of such seemingly simple tasks. Then, let them try to give the steps as clearly as possible. This exercise can be done by asking for volunteers from the whole class, or it can be done in small groups.

UNIT 8

What do you think?

Setting the Scene

Have the students look at the picture at the beginning of Unit 8. *What are the people doing*? (Introduce the vocabulary items *panel discussion* and *panelist*) *What is a panel discussion? What kinds of topics are discussed? Do the panelists usually reach a unanimous decision on a topic?*

Vocabulary

It may be necessary to go over the following additional vocabulary items:

impressions: as used in this conversation, ideas about a topic

superficial: dealing only with the surface, without depth

form: as used in this conversation, type or kind

today's: current

Listening

1. Play or read the conversation for the first time.
2. Ask the students what the subject of the panel discussion is. (*today's television*) Have the students write *TV in the U.S.* at the top of a piece of paper. Tell them to listen for the people's opinions and to jot down a few words to express each idea. (They should not worry about spelling.)
3. Play or read the conversation a second and a third time.
4. Have the students compare their notes in small groups and then have one or two groups give their list of comments.
   Answers:
   1) Today's television
   2) too violent
   3) too many police shows
   4) not enough educational programs
   5) news shows are superficial
   6) news reports are excellent
   Students may have any of these answers or all of them when they finish their group work.
5. Ask the students to point out the conflicting ideas which they heard. Example: *News reports are superficial. – News reports are excellent.*
6. Ask the students about the language and attitude they understood from the conversation. *Was it informal or formal? Did everyone agree with everyone else? How did they express their disagreement?* It may be necessary to have the students hear the last part of the conversation in which disagreement is expressed by, *Oh, I don't know about that.* and *Maybe, but . . . .* You may wish to point out to the students that in contrast to some cultures where it is considered impolite to openly express disagreement with other people, in English-speaking countries, no personal offense is taken if conflicting ideas are expressed during a discussion as long as it is done politely.

GIVE IT A TRY

1. Asking and giving opinions

▶ What do you think of today's TV programs?

▷ Well, if you ask me, they're terrible. Most of the programs are a complete waste of time.

Pronunciation: intonation of *if* clauses

Note that each clause has a strong stress accompanied by a rise and fall of the voice.

Play or read the dialog. Draw attention to the intonation in the second line, including the variations in the student book:

▷ Well, as far as I'm concerned . . .

▷ Well, I think . . .

Have students practice the intonation of these lines and then the entire dialog, including the alternative sentences in their books.

Of Interest

In some cultures it is not customary to express strong opinions openly, especially with strangers. However, people in the U.S. generally value an open exchange of ideas as long as 1) the subject is neutral and not personal and 2) as the speaker is careful in his/her choice of phrasing, and tone of voice. Even if a speaker is sure of an opinion, he/she will sometimes choose to express it as if it were just a possibility to avoid sounding like a "know-it-all." Such phrases as *I think* are often used to show that what is said is opinion rather than fact.

Practice 1

Group work. Divide the class into groups of three or four. Encourage all students to both ask and answer the questions. Also encourage them to elaborate on their opinions by giving examples or explanations.

Extension

After the students have discussed the topic in groups, have a class discussion about television in your country.

Practice 2

Pair work or group work. Divide the topics among the pairs or groups and encourage the students to elaborate on their opinions with examples or explanations. Then have the pairs or groups tell their opinions and explanations to the rest of the class. Ask the other class members for their opinions on the topic.

2. Agreeing with an opinion

▶ They're terrible.

▷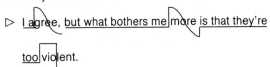
I agree, but what bothers me more is that they're too violent.

Pronunciation: intonation in sentences with more than one main thought group

Every major point a speaker wishes to make is marked by a strong sentence stress and accompanying rise in intonation.

Play or read the dialog. Draw attention to the intonation of the second line and that of the alternative lines in the Student Book:

I think so, too, and besides, they're not educational enough.

Have students practice saying their lines, trying out different combinations, being sure to give each thought group appropriate intonation.

Practice 1

Group work. Divide the class into small groups. Have the students rotate the parts of A, B, and C. Have the students practice with the information in their book, and then encourage them to use the same topics in their "real" situation. They might also add some other topics such as the room they're in, the building, and the area around them. As you walk around the room and monitor the groups, encourage the students to use all the alternative language forms presented in the model section.

Practice 2

Group work. Have the students rotate the parts of A, B, and C. After they have practiced with the information in the book, have them choose two or three places with which all the group members are familiar and give their opinions of those places, using the pattern in this practice exercise. Then have each group perform their new dialog for the rest of the class and ask the other class members if they agree.

3. Expressing a negative opinion

▶
There are too many police shows and not enough educational programs.

Pronunciation: review of intonation in sentences with more than one thought group

Play or read the above line. Draw attention to the intonation shown above and then ask the students how they would say the alternate line in their books.

(There is too much advertising and not enough entertainment.)

Ask the students if they know why *many* is used with *police shows* (it is a countable noun) and why *much* is used with *advertising* (it is a non-count noun). Students should be aware of these differences throughout this exercise.

Practice 1

Class work. List the topics in the book on the board and ask the students for other topics a local politician might ask about. Try to get at least four more topics. Then choose three students who will act as a group of politicians in front of the class. They will not have their books and should know the introductory question forms *How do you feel about . . .* and *What do you think of . . .* Have each "politician" ask about two or three of the topics. When the answers are given, the other "politicians" will take notes on the opinions given. When all topics are finished, the politicians should confirm their understanding by saying *So you think the bus system is pretty bad. There are too many delays and not enough buses. Is that right?*

Vocabulary

You may need to go over the following vocabulary items before the students do the exercise.

redevelopment: as used in this unit, improvement of a city area by fixing up old buildings and other means

recreational facilities: sports facilities such as swimming pools, basketball courts, etc.

Practice 2

Pair work. Each student should take notes on what his/her partner says. Then have three or four students tell the rest of the class about his/her partner's vacation. Encourage them to use structures such as *He/She thought the hotels were small and expensive, but the scenery was wonderful.*

4. Disagreeing

▶ In my opinion, the news shows are extremely superficial.

▷ I don't know about that. I think they're excellent.

Pronunciation: special intonation

The second line can be said more than one way. The intonation shown above is the least aggressive and, therefore, a good choice when trying to disagree in a friendly way.
    Play or read the dialog. Draw attention to the "friendly" intonation of *I don't know about that* and then consider the alternate sentences in the student book. *Do you think so?* (with normal intonation) is always an inoffensive way to disagree. The other alternatives can be said in more than one way, and the following intonation would sound the "friendliest":

I don't think so.

Oh, no.

Of Interest

I don't know about that is a polite form of *I disagree with you about that.*

Practice 1

Divide the class into small groups. Have them rotate the parts of A and B. After they have practiced the material in the book, have them express their opinions on the same subjects in their "real" situation.

Extension

After the groups have discussed the "real" topics, have a class discussion on the topics. Encourage the students to express their real opinions and give explanations or examples for their opinions.

Practice 2

Groups of three. First choose two students and model the conversation. As students practice in groups, have them rotate the roles. As you monitor the groups, help students with their intonation if necessary.

Extension

Have the students give their opinions of the topics listed in their "real" world. Again, encourage them to give explanations or examples. You may wish to do this as a class activity with as many students expressing their opinions as possible.

5. Qualifying a statement

▶ Presenting the news is what TV does best.

▷ That may be, but the news shows still aren't very good.

Pronunciation: review of intonation

Play or read the dialog. Draw attention to the intonation of the second line, and have students practice saying the dialog.

Of Interest

The phrase *That may be, but* is commonly used to show disagreement with the previous speaker's statement by adding some balancing statement which shows another aspect or viewpoint.

Practice 1

Pair work. Remind students to use the intonation they have just practiced in this exercise. As you circulate, provide any necessary help with it.

Extension

Ask the students for other topics on which people may have different viewpoints. You might refer them to topics previously discussed in this unit.

Practice 2

Pair or group work. If you wish to have the students work in groups, have the group do the exercise as a chain drill in which one student makes a suggestion, the next disagrees, the third makes another suggestion, etc.

Extension

Have each group develop a dialog similar to the one in the book but in which they are trying to decide what to do that evening or on the weekend.

LISTEN TO THIS

Part 1

1. Introduce the topic of gun control by asking the students if they or anyone they know owns a gun. Then ask general questions about the topic, such as *Why would someone want to own a gun? If you lived in a big city, why might you want to have one? Is it legal to have a gun (in your country)?*
2. Read the introductory material for Part 1. Then divide the class into groups of four or five students and give them 5–10 minutes to exchange ideas.
3. Ask one or two groups to tell the class their opinions and then ask the rest of the class to respond, both positively and negatively, using some of the language they have learned in this unit.

Part 2

1. Have the students read the instructions and look at the list.
2. Play or read the conversation the first time. Do not ask for the answers.
3. Play or read the conversation the second time. Give the students enough time to correct or complete the check list.
4. Have the students compare their lists in groups.

Answers:	For	Against
Paul		×
Jane	×	
Roger		×
Steven	×	
Susie		×

Part 3

1. Ask the students to give the reasons they heard in the conversation. List the opinions under *For* and *Against* on the board. You may need to play or read parts of the conversation again. Have the students give the ideas in their own words.
2. Class discussion or group work. Students can agree or disagree with the opinions they see on the board. Ask them to give explanations or examples for their opinions.

IF YOU HAVE TIME ...

Choose any issue(s) of current importance in the news and ask students to prepare to debate on either side of the issue(s). The preparation can be done partly as homework and partly in small groups with students sharing information. Divide the class into groups of six and assign three people in each group to defend one side of the issue and three to oppose. This can also be done as a presentation in front of the class.

UNIT 9

What did he do after getting his B.A.?

Setting the Scene

Have the students look at the picture at the beginning of Unit 9. Ask them questions about applications and qualifications. For example, *Have you ever filled out a job application? What kinds of questions are usually asked?*

Vocabulary

It may be necessary to review the following vocabulary items:

edit: prepare (another person's) writing for publication

Peace Corps: a U.S. volunteer organization which sends people to developing nations to aid in development projects

free-lance: a writer, artist, etc. who works from his/her own office or studio and does work for a variety of contractors

recruiter: a person whose job is to get new people to join an organization or company

Listening

1. Play or read the conversation the first time.
2. Write the following questions on the board:
   a) What is the applicant's name? (*Colson*)
   b) What type of business did he apply to? (*newspaper*)
   c) What type of work did he do in college? (*edited a magazine*)
   d) What did he do in Thailand? (*taught English/Peace Corps*)
   e) What has he been doing for the past four years? (*free-lance journalism*)
3. Follow steps 4–12 outlined on p. 2.

GIVE IT A TRY

1. Asking whether someone has done something

▶ Have you looked at this application yet?

Option 1
▷ Yeah, I've just read it.

Option 2
▷ No, I haven't read it yet.

Pronunciation: special intonation

Yes-no questions are most commonly said with rising intonation, but other patterns are possible. In the first sentence note the speaker's use of rising-falling intonation on the word *this* to show contrast between *this application* and others they have seen.

Play or read the dialog, drawing attention to this pattern. Then have students practice saying each line, including the alternative lines in their books. Listen to their intonation and provide help if necessary.

Of Interest

a) The present perfect tense is used here to talk about *non-specific* or *general* times in the past. You may wish to point out to the students that the simple past tense is used to speak about a *specific* time in the past. For example, *Have you ever gone skiing?* (at *any* time in the past) *Did you go skiing last year?* (a specific time is referred to)

b) You may wish to remind the students that *yet* may be used in the question and the negative statement but not in the affirmative statement.

c) *Just* refers to a time in the immediate past. *Already* is more general and may refer to any time in the past.

Practice 1 and 2

Pair work. Have the students switch parts for both Practice exercises. As you walk around and monitor the pairs, you may need to help students with the pronunciation of *I've*.

Practice 3

Pair work or group work. Encourage each pair or group to add additional questions about the trip. For example, *taken money out of the bank*, *made all the hotel reservations*, etc. After the students have done the exercise, have each pair or group ask its additional questions and have students from the other groups answer them.

2. Talking about habitual actions in the past

▶ Has he (ever) worked on a newspaper (before)?

Option 1
▷ No, but he used to edit a magazine when he was in college.

Option 2
▷ Yes, he edited the school newspaper when he was in college.

Pronunciation: blending of *has he*

In rapid speech, *has he* is pronounced /ha-ze/ or /ze/.

Play or read the dialog. Draw attention to the rapid pronunciation of *has he*. Have students use /ha-ze/ as they practice saying the lines.

> **Of Interest**
>
> In *He worked for the International Tribune in 1983*, the simple past tense is used because a specific time (in 1983) is used.

Practice 1

Pair work. Model questions and answers 1 and 2 so that students can hear both positive and negative responses. As you monitor the pairs give any necessary help with the past tense.

Extension

Have one or two students ask the questions, but not in the order they appear in the book. The other students should cover the questions and give the correct response.

Practice 2

Pair work or group work. Have each pair or group make up some additional questions about the past and answer them.

Extension

After the students have done the exercise in pairs or groups, have the students ask their other classmates the questions, including their additional questions.

3. Describing past events in sequence

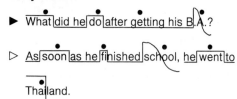

Pronunciation: review of stress, rhythm and intonation

Play or read the dialog. Then have students say it, including the variations in their books. These lines provide a good opportunity for students to review stress, rhythm and intonation and to work on fluency. The first line in particular is fun to practice at a rapid pace.

> **Of Interest**
>
> The second line of the above model can also be said with the sentence parts reversed: *He went to Thailand as soon as he finished school.* Encourage students to try shifting other sentences in this same way. This will expand the variety in their language.

Practice 1

Pair work.

Extension

Have the students make up some other "former classmates" and create a series of serious or amusing events for them after they graduated.

Practice 2

Pair work. Before students actually do the exercise, have them look over their parts in order to decide which verb they will use. Then, as they role-play, encourage them to "read and look up."

Practice 3

Pair work or group work. Students can use any set of experiences they choose. For example, an interesting five-year period in their lives, a two-week vacation, a particularly eventful day. As you walk around and monitor the students, encourage the questioners to use such phrases as: *Is that right? No kidding? You don't say*, and encourage the narrator to use such transitions as: *First, Then, After that*, etc.

Extension

Invite one or two students to share their experiences with the class and have the other students in the class ask about the events.

4. Describing concurrent past events

▶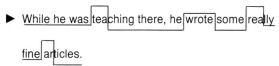
While he was teaching there, he wrote some really fine articles.

Pronunciation: review of intonation

Play or read the dialog. Ask students if they noticed how many times the voice rose and on which words. Then have them practice saying the line, using the same intonation as the model.

Practice 1

Class work. Have students draw a pencil line from a phrase in Column 1 to one in Column 2. Then have different students read their sentences. Several combinations are possible with some of the phrases, so ask for as many as students can come up with. Also, use the sentences to practice shifting the two parts of the sentence. For example, if a student gives a sentence *While she was skiing in the Alps, she had her passport stolen from her hotel room*, ask another student to give the sentence so that it begins with *She had . . .*

Practice 2

Pair work. Have each partner give the first comment for two or three of the pictures and have the other partner give an appropriate response, adding as much information as possible. As you monitor the pairs, see that students are using the past continuous and simple past tenses correctly. Encourage them to try shifting the order of the sentences.

Practice 3

Group work and class work. Divide the students into groups of three or four for the exercise. Have them exchange the information and add three or four questions of their own.

5. Describing what someone has been doing

▶ What's he been doing since then?

▷ He's been working as a freelance journalist.

Pronunciation: contrastive stress

In this model, *since* is stressed to emphasize the contrast between the past time period and the one *since then* that the speaker is interested in.

Play or read the dialog. Draw attention to the stress and intonation used in the first sentence. Then have students practice the dialog.

In Practice 1 which follows, *since* begins a clause, and the stress falls on the last stressed word in the clause. Illustrate this for students: *What's Jane been doing since she got her divorce?*

Of Interest

The present perfect continuous tense is commonly used to refer to actions which started at some time in the past and which continue into the present. A time-line might help to explain this. For example:

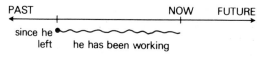

Practice

Pair work and class work. Have the students do the exercise in pairs. Then have them make up questions and answers about people in the news or in their countries. As you monitor the pairs, help students with intonation and help them also distinguish between single completed actions and continuous actions. Then have the students ask and answer the new questions as a class.

LISTEN TO THIS

1.

a. Have the students look at the directions and list for Listening 1. Go over any necessary vocabulary items.

b. Play or read the conversation the first time and

have the students check as many items as possible.
c. Play or read the conversation the second time and have the students check or complete the work.
d. Have the students check their work in small groups and then ask individual students for what has or has not been done.

Answers:

	done	not done
visited the museum		×
taken a bus tour		×
been to the zoo	×	
seen the art gallery		×
tried the sea food	×	

2.

a. Have the students look at the directions and list for Listening 2. Explain any necessary vocabulary items.
b. Play or read the conversation the first time and have the students draw as many lines as they can.
c. Play or read the conversation the second time and have the students check or complete the work
d. Have the students check their work in small groups and then ask individual students for the information.

Answers:
Richard Thomas – working in New York
Bobbie Worth – living in France
Ellen Rosenberg – working in Boston
Dan Collins – working in Chicago
Carol Chin – studying in Texas

IF YOU HAVE TIME ...

The practice exercises in this unit may lead to some real conversation among students. Let them talk freely in small groups. If they need prompting, suggest they talk about things they liked/disliked a lot when they were younger but may no longer feel the same way about. Or, suggest they talk about things they used to think were important which may no longer seem so important.

Variations — UNIT 10 — Variations

1. Around the world

a. If there are students from different countries in the class or if some member of the class has traveled to other countries, have the students ask them questions about customs in those other countries. This can be done as a class activity.

b. When the students have finished the exercise, have them compare and discuss their answers with the whole class.

2. A Radio-Call-in Show

a. Choose a student to act as the "host" of the program and give him/her time to look over the introductory remarks. At the same time, assign problems in the book to various members of the class. Have the students make up other problems which they would like the panel to give advice about. These may be serious or amusing. You may wish to bring in some problems from the advice column in your local newspaper as examples or distribute them to the class and have them ask the panel for their suggestions.

b. When the panel is giving advice, one or several members can offer suggestions for the same problems.

3. This is Your Life

a. Before the students do the activity, have them look over the information and make suggestions for other points of information they might want to ask about.

b. Have the students work in pairs or in groups of three or four and exchange information about themselves. Encourage them to ask for details about the information given. For each person who speaks, a different member of the group can take notes and then use these notes later to tell the class about their classmate.

Alternate activity

Students take the parts of other real or imaginary characters and tell about their lives. These may be serious or amusing. For example, Adam and Eve, a famous king or queen, or a movie star. As they tell the story of their lives, encourage the other students to ask for explanations or more details.

4. Cooking Corner

Have the students work in groups of three or four. As one person speaks, the other students should take notes and then compare their notes for accuracy. If the students are from different countries, ask them to give the recipe for a traditional national dish.

Extension

Have some students describe other processes such as how to apply for a visa, how to develop film, how to change a tire on a car, etc.

5. A Reader Survey

a. Only the student who is asking the questions should look at the survey questions. Remind the students that in asking questions for a survey, the interviewer makes frequent use of indirect question forms such as *Could you tell me . . . .*

b. Have the students compare the results of the survey and describe the "average" reader of the magazine.

Extension

You may wish to divide the class into groups and have each group develop a survey for different government departments. These can be real or imaginary. For example, the Transportation Department, the Department of Economic Affairs, the Department of Consumer Affairs, the Department of Education, the Department of Culture and Entertainment. Then have the students use their surveys with other members of the class.

6. Politics as Usual

a. Divide the class into groups of four or six. Have half the students ask the questions and the other half answer. Encourage the students to ask questions about other important issues of the day such as the oil situation, the nuclear arms race, environmental pollution, etc.

b. Have different commentators take notes on the responses on different topics and then report them to the rest of the class.

Alternate activity

Have a "press conference," in which three or four "candidates" are interviewed by the rest of the class. Have the interviewers make up some questions based on recent issues of interest.

UNIT 11

What are you going to do?

Setting the Scene

Have the students look at the picture at the beginning of Unit 11. Tell them that the person in the picture is a guidance counselor, a person in high schools who helps a student decide what career to follow and how to plan for it. This includes deciding about colleges or other schools.

Vocabulary

The students may need to review the following vocabulary items.

major: The main subject someone studies while in college. Usually in the first two years of college, students take general courses, and in the last two they concentrate on their major field.

field: area of study or work

postpone: delay until some future time

Money is pretty tight: People don't have much money to spend.

scholarship: money given by a government, school, or organization to students for their studies. A scholarship usually depends on a student's financial need and academic ability.

GIVE IT A TRY

1. Asking about future plans (1)

▶ What are you going to do after you graduate?

Option 1
▷ I'm planning to go to college

Option 2
▷ I don't know yet.

Pronunciation: blending of *going to* reviewed

Play or read the dialog. Draw attention to the rapid speech pronunciation of *going to* /gonna/ and have students practice using it in a shortened version of the first line (*What are you going to do?*) until they are comfortable with it. Then add on the extra words *after you graduate*, and have students work on stress and rhythm.

Of Interest

In the opening conversation, there are several expressions used to refer to the future.

1. *Planning to* do something is more concrete than thinking about doing something.
2. In *if* clauses, future meaning is most commonly expressed by the word *will*. In other cases, *going to* is more frequently used.
3. When a time expression is given or understood, we often use the present continuous tense to speak of definite plans for the immediate future. For example, *I'm having dinner with my family tonight.* or *I'm working with my father tomorrow.* In these cases the *going to* future could also be used.

Practice 1

Have students talk in groups of three or four. Encourage them to use *What are you planning to do*, *What are you going to do*, and *What are you doing* interchangeably.

Practice 2

Pair work. Have the students "read and look up."

Extension

After the students have practiced the dialog, have them make up another activity they are planning to do and use the dialog given as a model. They may choose any activity which they might really plan to do. For example, *go dancing*, *go to a football game*. After they have practiced the new dialog, have one of the students take the part of Student A and try the dialog with another student in class.

2. Asking about future plans (2)

▶ What do you plan to study there?

Option 1
▷ I'm thinking of majoring in chemistry.

Option 2

▷ I haven't made up my mind yet.

Pronunciation: review of intonation

Play or read the dialog. Ask students how they think each sentence should be read. Confirm (or correct) the models they suggest and then have them practice the dialogs, including the variations in their books, working on speed and fluency.

Of Interest

The word *want* is not used in the present continuous tense (*I want*, but not *I am wanting*.) In contrast, *plan* and *intend* can be used both in the simple present and in the present continuous. (*I plan; I am planning*.)

Practice 1 and 2

Pair work. If there is time, have students make up several more questions to ask each other.

3. Asking about Future Plans (3)

▶ What are you planning to do?
▷ I'm hoping to go to Europe.

Pronunciation: blending of *What are you*

In rapid speech, *What are you* sounds like /wuh-der-yuh/.
Play or read the dialog. Draw attention to the blending described and to the stress pattern of the sentence. Have students practice the dialog including the variations in their books.

Practice 1 and 2

Pair work.

Extension

Have one of the students from each group give some information to the class about one or two members of his/her group. *Or* have students from different groups take the part of Student A and Student B. Then ask the rest of the class to give the information they heard.

4. Describing changes in plans

▶ What do you think you're going to do?
▷ I was thinking of going to college, but I might have to get a job instead.

Pronunciation: blending of *going to* reviewed

Play or read the dialog. Ask students how *going to do* and *going to go* are pronounced in rapid speech. /gonna do, gonna go/ (*Going to* is not reduced in the second sentence since it is used as a main verb.) Then have them practice saying each line as rapidly and rhythmically as possible, working on a phrase at a time.

Practice 1

Pairs. After students do the exercise, have them make up similar sentences of their own.

Practice 2 and 3

Pair work.

5. Explaining Possibilities

▶ And what are you going to do?

Option 1

▷ If I get a scholarship, I'll study architecture.

Option 2

▷ If I don't get a scholarship, I suppose I'll get a job.

Pronunciation: Contrastive stress

Note how in the second speaker's second sentence, *don't* is stressed in order to make clear the contrast between the two possibilities.
Play or read the dialog. Draw attention to the stress and intonation the second speaker uses. Have students practice saying the sentences, including the variations in their books.

> **Of Interest**
>
> In future conditional sentences, the clause beginning with *if* is always in the present tense; the other clause expresses future, usually using *will* or, less frequently, other modal auxiliaries (*can*, *may*, etc.).

Practice 1

Pair work. As you walk around the room and monitor the students, pay particular attention to the use of the present tense in the *if* clause and the use of *will* or appropriate alternatives in the main clause.

Practice 2

Divide the class into groups of three (four if necessary). One student will be the travel agent. Have students switch parts and ask for information about different places on the chart.

LISTEN TO THIS

1.

a. Have the students read the directions. Then have them write down the days of the week on a piece of paper and leave room next to each for Monica's plans that evening.
b. Play or read the conversation the first time and have the students write down as much as they understand.
c. Play or read the conversation the second time and have the students complete or check their lists.
d. Have the students compare their lists in small groups. Then ask individual students to tell Monica's plans for each evening.

Answers:
Monday – finish term paper
Tuesday – (help roommate) clean the apartment
Wednesday – have company
Thursday – take father out for dinner
Friday – go to concert with Peter

2.

a. Have the students read the directions. Then have them write down the names of the people in the conversation on a piece of paper. (See below)
b. Go over the menu, explaining any unknown vocabulary and pronouncing the items.
c. Play or read the conversation the first time. Have students write down the food choice next to the name of the character.
d. Play or read the conversation the second time and have the students complete or check their list.
e. Have the students compare their answers in small groups. Then have someone write the correct answers on the board.

Answers:
Barbara – chicken (Kiev)
John – chicken (Kiev)
Ellen – fish (flounder)
Tony – cheese omelette
Peter – steak

IF YOU HAVE TIME ...

Ask students to imagine they are going to be given a million dollars. There is only one problem: They have to use it all within two weeks. They are not allowed to put any of it into a bank. Have them tell each other what they will do with the money first and so on. For example, "First, I'm going to take my parents out for an elegant dinner and ask them for their advice. Then, I'm going to buy a new car. After that, I think I'll ...."

UNIT 12

Did you hear what happened?

Setting the Scene

Have the students look at the picture at the beginning of the unit. Ask: *What is going on in this picture*? (Two women are talking.) In this conversation one woman tells the other some bad news. *What can you say in English when you hear bad news*? (Accept any responses that are possible and write them on the board.) *Now, listen to how the woman in the conversation does it, and how the other responds.*

Vocabulary

The students may have to review the following vocabulary items:

temperature: body heat (in this conversation)

cholera: A disease caused by unclean food or water. Cholera can be fatal.

I gather: I understand from the things I have heard.

apparently: it seems

complications: new difficulties which may develop when someone is ill

Listening

1. Play or read the conversation for the first time.
2. Write the following statements on the board:
    a) Ron has a high temperature. (True)
    b) He may have malaria. (False)
    c) Maybe he got the disease in Malaysia. (False)
    d) He went to see the doctor quite a while ago. (False)
    e) Ron's health is getting better. (True)
    f) He should only be in the hospital for a few days. (False)

    Students can prepare an answer sheet and write *True* or *False* for each question.
3. Play the tape or read the conversation for the second time, and if necessary, a third.
4. Check the answers. If the answers are false, ask the students to supply the correct information.

GIVE IT A TRY

1. Responding to good and bad news

▶ Did you know that Ron was in the hospital?

▷

Pronunciation: intonation choices

The second speaker's line can be said as a question (shown above) or an exclamation:

Play or read the model. Draw attention to the intonation and have students practice the dialog, including the variations in their books.

Practice 1

Pair work. As you monitor the pairs, check to see that students are responding appropriately.

Extension

Have the students make up additional bits of news to which their partners can respond. For example, *Did you hear that Peter dropped out of school? Did you hear that there was a big fire downtown last night?*

Practice 2

Pair or group work. Encourage the students to respond appropriately to the news and then ask for more information. For example:
A: Barbara broke her leg.
B: Oh, that's too bad. How did it happen?
A: She fell down a flight of stairs.

Extension

Have each pair or group make up two or three additional bits of news based on their mutual interests or recent news items. The other students will respond appropriately. For example,
A: Did you hear that Peter dropped out of school?
B: Oh, really? When did that happen?
A: Last week, I think.

These exchanges can then be put on the blackboard for the class to see.

2. Suggesting how something probably occurred.

▶ Did you know that Ron had cholera?
▷ Oh really? How awful!
▶ Yeah. He just came back from India. He must have gotten it while he was there.

Pronunciation: blending of *must have*

In rapid speech, *must have* sounds like /mus-tuv/. (This occurs when *have* is used as an auxiliary.)
   Play or read the dialog. Draw attention to the pronunciation of *must have*. Have students practice saying the third line and then the whole dialog, including the variations in their books.

Of Interest

Must have + past participle is used for past probability.

Practice 1

Pair work or group work.

Extension

Have each pair or group make up a situation similar to those in the exercise. They will present the situation to the rest of the class and other students will suggest the probable cause. For example:
A: *Hashim had an important math exam yesterday, and he seems very happy today.*
B: *He must have done well on his exam.*

Practice 2

1. Group work. Divide the class into groups of three and have the students read the newspaper articles silently. You can either assign all articles to all groups or assign one or two articles to each group.
2. After the students read the articles, they will make suggestions and observations using *He/She might have . . . . He/She should have . . . .*
3. Have the students compare their answers with other groups. If different articles are assigned to each group, have one group member read the article and have the other members give their observations and suggestions. Ask other members if they agree with the ideas or if they can give others.

Possible answers:
a) He might have gotten drunk at the party. He shouldn't have driven home.
b) The thief might have hidden in the storage room. The guards should have checked more carefully.
c) The passenger might have fainted from the heat. They should have fixed the air conditioning immediately.
d) The electrical wiring might have started the fire. They should have fixed it much earlier.
e) The tiger might have jumped over the fence. They should have built it higher.

3. Saying what someone should have done

▶ He only went to see the doctor last week.
▷ He should have seen a doctor earlier.

Pronunciation: blending of *should have*

In rapid speech, *should have* is pronounced /shu-duv/ and sometimes even /shu-duh/. Similarly, *shouldn't have* sounds like /shu-du-nuv/.
   Play or read the dialog. Ask students how they think *should have* sounds in rapid speech. Confirm (or correct) their observation. Have them practice using /shu-duv/ and /shu-du-nuv/ as they go through the dialog and variations.

Of Interest

Should(n't) have or *ought to have* + past participle are used to give advice about the past.

Practice 1

Pair work. As you monitor the pairs encourage them to use a variety of responses to the situation. For example, *Really? Oh, that's too bad. Oh, how awful.* etc.

Extension

Have each pair develop two or three other problems that should have been taken care of before the Smiths left for vacation. Then have them present the problems to the rest of the class for appropriate responses.

Practice 2

Pair work or group work. Have the students develop two possible responses to the situation. Then compare the responses of different pairs or groups in the class.

Did you hear what happened?

Extension

Have the pairs or groups develop two other problem situations the Roberts encountered. Have the rest of the class offer advice about what they might have done to prevent the problem.

4. Suggesting a course of action

▶ If he|stays|in the|hospital for a few weeks, he

should|be able to avoid complications.

Pronunciation: review of stress, rhythm and intonation

This model can be used to review stress, rhythm, and intonation. Play or read the above line. Ask students where the voice rises (*hospital* and *complications*). Have them practice each half of the sentence and then put them together, working on fluency as well as correct stress, rhythm and intonation.

Of Interest

The way *should* and *ought* to are used here, they indicate probability. Students are probably familiar with other meanings of these modal auxiliaries and may be surprised to see the way they are used here. It may be useful to write a paraphrase of the model:
He should be able to avoid complications.
He'll probably be able to avoid complications.

Practice 1

Pair work.

Practice 2

Group work and class work. Have the students work in groups to give advice for each problem. Then have the groups compare their solutions in a class discussion.

LISTEN TO THIS

1.

a. Have the students read the directions.
b. Go over the list of possible reasons and explain any necessary vocabulary items.
c. Play or read the conversation the first time. Have the students check the appropriate answer.
d. Play or read the conversation the second time.
e. Have students check their answers in small groups.

Answer:
The subway must be late.

2.

a. Have the students read the directions and look at the pictures. Ask them the location of each picture.
b. Play or read the conversation the first time. Students should put a check (✓) next to the answer they choose.
c. Play or read the conversation the second time. This time students can confirm or correct their answer.
d. Ask for the correct answer.

Answer:
the book shop

IF YOU HAVE TIME ...

1. Have each pair verbalize two or three complaints they have in their personal, professional, or academic lives. Then have each pair present the problems to the class and have the other class members give appropriate advice. The problems and the advice may be serious or amusing.

UNIT 13

What's this for?

Setting the Scene
Have students look at the picture. Ask them: *What do you think they are saying*? As students offer possibilities, write these lines in the form of a dialog on the board, helping with the language where needed.

Vocabulary
If this vocabulary has not already come up, you can point out the meanings of these words using these definitions and the photo in the Student Book.

handle: the part of an object which is specially made for holding it

vacuum cleaner: (use photo)

dust: fine, dry dirt

dust bag: a bag inside or attached to a vacuum cleaner which collects dust

clip: a small plastic or metal object for holding things together

press down: push down

lift off: take off, remove

bent: at an angle or curved

Listening
1. Play or read the conversation for the first time. As the description is given, point to the part mentioned in the photo.
2. Write the following phrases on the board. Have the students write them on a piece of paper and then listen for the order in which they hear each action.
   lift off the back   (3)
   turn off the power   (1)
   take out the dust bag   (4)
   press down the clip   (2)
3. Play or read the conversation the second time. As they listen, the students can number the steps.
4. Now write these questions on the board and go over any vocabulary that students may not know.
   Why is the handle bent? (So you can clean under furniture easily.)
   Is the vacuum cleaner heavy or light? (Light.)
   Why? (It's made of plastic./It's plastic.)
   When can they deliver it? (Tomorrow morning.)

   deliver: bring to someone's house
5. Play or read the conversation a third time.
6. Have students check their answers in small groups.
7. Write the answers on the blackboard.

GIVE IT A TRY

1. Describing what objects are used for
▶ What's this thing for?
▷ That's for picking up heavy dirt.

Pronunciation: stressed and reduced forms of *for*

In the second line *for* is said very quickly and reduced to /fer/, which is usual for function words. In the first line, where *for* means *used for*, it is said with more emphasis.
Play or read the dialog. Ask students to listen to rhythm and the pronunciation of *for* in each line and draw their attention to the difference. Then have them practice saying the dialog.

> **Of Interest**
>
> The phrase *It's used to* is followed by the simple form of the verb *pick up*. The phrase *It's used for* is followed by the gerund *picking up*. Both have the same meaning.

Practice 1
Pair, group, or class work. Tell students to use both *It's used to . . .* and *It's used for . . .* As you circulate, you may need to help students understand and pronounce the cues.

Practice 2
Pair work. Have Student A cover the picture and wording used by Student B. Student B must look to see which part Student A is pointing at or referring to.

Extension
If you have pictures of other common appliances, divide them among the class and have the students figure out the functions of different parts. If you have a camera or the booklet for any electrical appliance, students could also use them for this exercise.

What's this for?

2. Explaining the reasons for certain features

▶ Why is it bent?
▷ That's so you can clean under furniture more easily.

Pronunciation: blending of *Why is it*

In rapid speech *Why is it* sounds like /wi-zit/. Play or read the dialog. Draw attention to the blending described. Then have students practice saying the lines using either blended form.

> **Of Interest**
>
> The phrase *That's so ...* means *The purpose of that is so ...*

Practice

Pair work. Students use the ads as cues, making necessary changes in the language. For example:
folding mattress – *That's so you can store it more easily.*
cassette player with removable plastic door – *That's so you can clean it more easily.*
frying pan – *That's so you can cook faster.* or *That's so you can clean it easier.*

3. Explaining how to do things (1)

▶ First you have to make sure (that) the power has been turned off.

▷ Then what do I do?

Pronunciation: intonation to show connections

In the second line, the voice rises and falls on *Then*. By doing this the speaker connects his sentence to the previous one (*First ... Then*).
Play or read the dialog. Ask students to say the second line the way the speaker did. (Correct them if necessary.) Draw attention to the connection between *First* and *Then*. Then have students practice the dialog. Continue working on intonation with the sentences in Practice 1 below. Write them on the board and ask students where they think the major stresses should fall. They will see that the words *first* and *then* continue to be stressed, as does the similar expression *after that*. (Note that the stress in *after that* falls on *that*.)

> **Of Interest**
>
> When we give directions, we can use the passive voice (*Make sure that the power has been turned off*) or the active voice (*Make sure that you turn off the power.*) For practice purposes, the passive voice has been used in this exercise.

Practice 1

Pair work. Do the exercise orally, or have Student B describe the steps and have Student A write them down on a piece of paper. Then have both students check the steps which Student A has written.

Practice 2

Pair work or group work. If a cassette recorder, camera, or instruction booklet with pictures are available, divide them among the class and have each group or pair develop a description of the necessary steps for using the item. Then have the pairs or groups explain the procedure to the rest of the class.

4. Explaining how to do things (2)

▶ First this clip is pressed down.

Then the back is lifted off. And finally the dust bag is removed.

Pronunciation: review of stress in two word verbs

In *pressed down* and *lifted off*, the particles *down* and *off* are stressed more than the verbs they follow.
Play or read the above lines. Draw attention to the stress on the particles. Then have students practice saying the lines. These sentences also offer an opportunity to review the intonation pattern learned in the preceding model with *First*, *Then* and *finally*.

Practice

Pair work. Have only Student A look at the first set of pictures. Have that student describe the steps to the other student, who will write down the steps as they are given. Then have both students look only at the pictures (not the words below) to see that the other student has written and understood the steps. Follow the same procedure for the use of a coffee maker.

Extension

Have the students give a similar description of a simple recipe or device. For example, how to make a hamburger, how to make rice, how to operate a can opener. Or have the students bring in a similar description of a simple device or recipe.

5. Describing where things were made and what they are made of

▶ Could you tell me what this is made of?

And do you know where it was made?

Pronunciation: review of stress and rhythm

This model can be used to practice stressing content and *Wh-* words and reducing function words. Stresses occuring at regular intervals as they do here produce the rhythm characteristic of English.

Play or read the lines. Ask students which words are stressed. Tap out the rhythm and have them say the lines, working on speed and fluency. *Could you tell me* should be pronounced as a single word with the stress on *tell*. *Do you know* is a similar case, with the stress on *know*.

Practice

Pair work. Have Student A look only at the pictures without the information. Students can switch roles after the first three items so that both have a chance to ask and answer.

Extension

Have the students look through their possessions to find any articles which have labels describing material and/or origin. (For example, a wallet, a purse, a watch, gloves.) Then have other students ask the questions. If not all the information can be found, ask the students for the response they would give. (Example: *I'm sorry, but I don't know where it was made.*)

6. Finding out whether something can be done

▶ Can it be delivered?
▷ Sure, we can deliver it tomorrow.

Pronunciation: review of the reduced form of *can*

This model can be used to review the reduction of *can* to /kin/ in rapid speech. Play or read the model. Ask students how *can* is pronounced in rapid speech. Then have them practice the dialog, using the reduction.

> **Of Interest**
>
> Both the question and the answer can be in the active or passive voice. For example, *Can it be delivered?* or *Can you deliver it? We can deliver it tomorrow.* or *It can be delivered tomorrow.* In these situations, the voices are often mixed.

Practice 1

Group work. Divide the class into groups of three or four. Have the students look at the information which is provided and make up questions about each item. (Some of these questions will be answered in the negative: *No. You can't wash ....*) Tell the students to use questions and answers in both the active and passive voices.

Practice 2

Pair work. Student B answers *Yes* or *No* and gives additional information if the answer is *No*.

Answers:
– Woolens shouldn't be washed in a washing machine. They should be washed in cool water by hand.
– Bananas should be kept outside a refrigerator.
– Fish can be kept in a freezer.
– They can be grown outdoors only if the weather is warm all year round. Otherwise, they should be grown indoors.
– Saucepans should not be washed in a dishwasher. They should be washed by hand.

LISTEN TO THIS

1.

a. Have the students read the instructions.
b. Then go over the list of materials with them. If any are new vocabulary items, illustrate by showing students objects in the classroom made of these materials or let them use bilingual dictionaries.
c. Play or read the conversation the first time. Have the students put a check (✓) next to each material on which the cleaner can be used.

d. Play or read the conversation a second time. Give the students time to complete or check their work.
e. Ask individual students to give the answer for individual materials.

Answers:
- _____ silver
- ✓ aluminum
- ✓ brass
- ✓ baths
- ✓ tiles
- _____ wood
- ✓ plastic

f. Ask the students if they remember the comments the clerk made about silver and wood. Answer: *There is a special cleaner for silver. The cleaner might ruin the wood.*
g. Ask the students for the statements used by the clerk in addition to or in place of *yes* and *no*. This will help the students develop a larger variety of responses.

Answers:
Yes, with certain kinds. It's very good on . . . .
Well, it's not really very good with . . . .
Yes, it works well on . . . .
Yes, it's perfect for . . . .
Plastic's fine. No trouble at all.

2.

a. Have the students look at the directions. Then have them look at the list of instructions for using the oven cleaners. Tell them that only a few of the items will be checked.
b. Explain any necessary vocabulary items.
   paste: (If paste is available, show it and explain that the word *paste* is also used for substances that are similarly thick.)
   spray: (Demonstrate the action of spraying making appropriate sound effects or let students use their dictionaries.)
c. Play or read the conversation for the first time. Tell the students to put a check next to the correct items.
d. Play the tape or read the conversation for the second time. Students should check or complete their answers.
e. Have the students compare their answers in small groups or ask individual students for each item.

IF YOU HAVE TIME . . .

Play "Twenty Questions." Model the game first. Tell students they can ask up to 20 questions to try and guess what object you are thinking of. The only answers you will give to the questions, however, are *yes* or *no*. Tell the students you are thinking of something found in a kitchen (a spoon). They should be encouraged to ask such questions as *Is the thing heavy? Is it made of cloth? Is it used for cooking?* etc. Now you can play the game either as a whole class activity or in groups of five or six. Have the person who is answering the questions write down the name of the thing the others are trying to guess.

UNIT 14

What did they say about Mexico?

Setting the Scene

Have the students look at the picture at the beginning of Unit 14. Tell them that the woman has just finished talking to her friend about the friend's visit to Mexico. Ask questions about the students' travel experiences. For example, *Has anyone been to (name of country)? What places have you traveled to? Did you have a good time? What was the weather like? Where did you stay? Did you make hotel reservations before you went?*

Vocabulary

You may need to review the following vocabulary items:

accommodations: hotel room

coast: the area near the sea

marvelous: wonderful

reservations: advance arrangements for a hotel room

Listening

1. Play or read the conversations the first time.
2. Put the following statements on the board. Tell the students to write *T* for *True* and *F* for *False* on their papers.
   a) The friends went to Mexico. (True)
   b) The weather in Mexico City was warm. (False)
   c) They only visited Mexico City while in Mexico. (False)
   d) The friends said that there was no need for reservations. (False)
   e) The cheapest hotels listed in the guide book were $25. (False)
3. Continue with steps 4–12 outlined on p. 2.

GIVE IT A TRY

1. Asking about what someone said (1)

▶ What did she say about Mexico?

▷ She said we'd really enjoy it.

Pronunciation: review of stress, intonation and rhythm

Play or read the dialog. Ask students which words are stressed and where the voice rises and falls. Then have them practice saying the lines including the variations, working on speed and fluency.

Of Interest

In reporting speech, when the present tense is used (*She says* . . .) there is no change in verb tenses from the original words. For example, *She says that we will enjoy it.* However, in reporting speech we usually use the past tense (*She said* . . .) which generally requires changes in the tenses:

Direct		Indirect
We *will* enjoy it	She said	we *would* enjoy it.
We *can* do it.	(that)	we *could* do it.
We *may* do it.		we *might* do it.
She *has* the money.		she *had* the money.
She *has seen* it.		she *had seen* it.
She *enjoyed* it.		she *had enjoyed* it.

Practice

Pair or group work. As you monitor the pairs or groups check to see that students are making the necessary changes.

Extension

Have students make two or three statements about a trip they have taken. Then ask other students. *What did (s)he say about the trip?*

2. Asking about what someone said (2)

▶ Did you ask how the weather was?

▷ It seems (that) it was cool in Mexico City.

Pronunciation: stress

A speaker will usually make new information more prominent by giving it the major stress. Thus, in the second line, *cool* rather than *Mexico City* receives the strongest stress.

Play or read the dialog. Ask students which word the voice rises on in each sentence. Then have them practice saying the lines, including the variations in their books.

Practice 1 and 2

Pair work or group work. Student A should take notes on a piece of paper.

3. Asking about what someone said (3)

Pronunciation: blending of *did she*

▶ Did she say if they reserved a room in advance?
▷ Apparently they did.

In rapid speech, *did she* is pronounced /dih-che/ or even /che/. Play or read the dialog. Draw attention to the blending of *did she,* which is especially important for listening comprehension. Then have students practice saying the lines, including the variations in their books.

> **Of Interest**
>
> When the original question does not begin with a question word such as *when, where, how,* etc., the indirect question begins with *if* or *whether.* For example, *Did you have a good time?* becomes *She asked me if (or whether) I had a good time.*

Practice 1 and 2

Groups of three. Follow the same procedure as in the preceding practice exercises. As you monitor the groups, check to see that students are making the necessary changes.

4. Reporting recommendations

▶ Did you ask about the hotels?
▷ Yes. She recommended that we make reservations.

Pronunciation: blending of *did you ask*

In rapid speech, *did you ask* is pronounced /juh-ask/ or even /j'ask/.
Play or read the dialog. Draw attention to the blending described and have students practice using the blended form as they say the lines.

> **Of Interest**
>
> 1. The words *recommended, suggested,* and *advised* have the same meaning in this context. In the clause which follows these words, the verb is always in the simple form (with no *-s*). For example, *He suggested that I/you/he/we/they do it immediately.* (It is incorrect to say *He suggested that we should do it* or *I suggested that he does it.*)
> 2. The words *recommend, suggest,* and *advise* are more formal in tone than *say* and *tell.* They are, therefore, more likely to be used in writing or formal speech.

Practice 1

Pair work. Have one student (Student A) play Lorraine. A second student (Student B) asks questions.

Practice 2

Pair work. Students exchange partners. Student A moves to work with a different Student B and asks the indirect questions.

5. Reporting information from a book

▶ What does it say about accommodations?
▷ It says (that) the cheapest is around thirty-five dollars.

Pronunciation: blending of *What does it*

In rapid speech, *What does it* sounds like /whu-duh-zit/ or even /wut-zit/.
Play or read the model. Draw attention to the blended forms and have students use /wuh-duh-zit/ as they practice saying the dialog, including the variations in their books.

Practice 1

Go over the following vocabulary items, if necessary.

beach bungalow: a small house located near the beach

rate of exchange: the difference in value between one currency and another

traveler's checks: checks issued by banks or companies (for example, American Express) which can be used the same as cash

caution should be exercised: be careful

Pair work. Student B reads the information about Mexico. Student A is unable to see this information and writes down on a piece of paper the answers given by Student B. After the students have finished the exercise, have the students who wrote down the answers check their information. If there are any differences, they should check the information again with Student B.

Extension

Brochures from different countries are easily available from most travel agencies. Bring in a number of them and divide them among groups in the class. Have each group get as much information as possible by using the questions throughout this unit. Then have the students exchange the information about the different countries.

Practice 2

Groups of three. Each student gives the information about one of the products. The other students write down or try to remember and repeat the information they hear.

Of Interest

In order to save space, labels give shortened versions of sentences. For example, *Apply directly to burned area* would normally be said as *Apply the cream directly to the burned area.* Show students how to change the shortened form to the more conversational form when they speak. Other examples on the labels in this exercise are *Repeat after four hours if necessary. (Repeat the dosage after four hours if it is necessary). Reapply every 3 or 4 hours. (Reapply the cream every 3 or 4 hours.)*

Extension

Bring in some medications with instructions in English. Divide the class into groups and give one medication to each group. Then have each group tell the class what the medication is for and what instructions need to be followed.

LISTEN TO THIS

1.

a. Have the students read the directions
b. Explain any necessary vocabulary items.
c. Play or read the conversation for the first time. Have the students put a check (✓) next to the correct answer.
d. Play or read the conversation the second time. Give the students time to complete or to check their work.
e. Check the answers to the comprehension exercise.

Answers:
1. the trip — very enjoyable
2. the weather — cool
3. the hotels — good and inexpensive
4. communication problems — some problems
5. hotel staff — very helpful
6. things to buy — jewelry

2.

a. Have the students read the directions.
b. Explain any necessary terms.
   carvings: decorative objects made of wood or other materials shaped by cutting with a knife.
c. Play or read the conversation for the first time. Have the students put a check (✓) next to the correct answer.
d. Play or read the conversation for the second time. Give the students time to complete or check their answers.
e. Check answers.

Answers:
You should change money — at a state bank
cholera — still a rash of cholera
visa — should get one before entering the country
things to buy — carvings and paintings
where to buy things — out of the capital
tours — to a volcano

IF YOU HAVE TIME...

If your students come from several countries or have traveled to other countries, ask some of them to act as "travel agents" for the others. Have students ask questions about travel to the various places.

Variations — UNIT 15 — Variations

1. Wedding plans

1. Have the students read the directions and look at the questions. You may need to review the following vocabulary items:

   bride: a woman on her wedding day

   bridegroom or *groom*: a man on his wedding day

   reception: a party held after a wedding

   best man: the man who supports the bridegroom during his wedding

   bridesmaid: A young, unmarried woman who helps the bride during her wedding. There can be several.

   honeymoon: a vacation, usually of one or two weeks, taken by the married couple immediately after the wedding

2. Divide the class into groups of three — the couple and the reporter. The couple can choose to be any real or imaginary couple. Have the couple look at the questions before the interview. During the interview, only the reporter should look at the questions. He/She should also take notes on the answers.

Extension

Choose two or three interesting couples and have the interviewer give a TV report on their plans.

2. A new car

1. Have the students look at the first picture. Point out examples of a *gauge,* a *switch,* and a *lever,* and help students pronounce these words. Have the students cover the second picture and try to figure out what the different parts are and what they are used for.
2. Divide the class into pairs and have the students do the activity. As you monitor the pairs, encourage the students to figure out what each object is from its name. Offer help as needed.

   Answer:

   ignition switch — uses a key to turn on the motor

   emergency flashing switch — turns on front and rear flashing lights when the driver wants to call attention to the car

   open door warning light — a light which turns on when the door is open

   fuel gauge — shows how much gasoline is in the tank

   air vent — allows air into the car

Extension

Many motorcycle and bicycle shops have brochures for their products. If possible, bring a few brochures to the class and have students identify the different parts of the motorcycle or bicycle and tell their use.

3. Bad news

1. Divide the class into groups of three or four and assign the first article to half of the groups and the second to the others. Each group must read its article, discuss it, and make a list of suggestions concerning it.
2. When the students have finished, have some students who read the first article explain it in their own words to the students who read the second article.
3. Have the groups give their suggestions. Some may be the same; some may be different. Ask the students who are listening whether they agree with the suggestions or have others to add.
4. Follow the same procedure with the students who have read the second article.

Extension

Take shortened versions of recent newspaper or magazine articles which describe similar disasters and explain them to the class. Have the students make suggestions about each situation.

4. A trip to Turkey

1. Divide the class into groups of three. Have two students make up and ask questions of the other. Give the students time to read over the information before they begin. Tell students to use such forms as *Can you tell me . . .? I'd like to know . . . I also want to find out . . .*
2. As the students do the activity, they should take notes on the information and then do the second half of the activity with Student C, the "travel agent," who will listen and make any necessary corrections in Student A's information.

Extension

Bring in brochures from other countries or cities or popular vacation places. Divide the class into small groups, distribute the brochures, and have them make up questions of interest to someone visiting those places. Then have them check the brochure for the information. The groups may then compare the different places and discuss where they might choose to visit. They can also talk about a place they might not want to visit.

5. The mail must go through

1. Divide the class into pairs. Have each student cover the pictures used by his/her partner. Remind the students that the process should be described in the passive voice. Give some examples if necessary.
2. As each student gives the steps involved in the process, the partner should repeat them for confirmation and take notes on them.

6. From the farm to your market

Students remain in pairs but switch roles so that those who were listeners in the last activity are now the ones to describe the process. Again, remind students to use the passive voice where possible.